ELEANOR ROOSEVELT

First Lady and Humanitarian

— PEOPLE TO KNOW —

ELEANOR ROOSEVELT

First Lady and Humanitarian

Michael A. Schuman

ENSLOW PUBLISHERS, INC.

44 Fadem Rd.	P.O. Box 38
Box 699	Aldershot
Springfield, N.J. 07081	Hants GU12 6BP
U.S.A.	U.K.

*To Trisha and Alexandra
and in memory of Kelila*

Library of Congress Cataloging-in-Publication Data

Schuman, Michael.
    Eleanor Roosevelt: first lady and humanitarian / Michael A. Schuman.
        p. cm. — (People to know)
    Includes bibliographical references (p.) and index.
    ISBN 0-89490-547-3
    1. Roosevelt, Eleanor, 1884-1962—Juvenile literature. 2. Presidents'
spouses—United States—Biography—Juvenile literature. I. Title. II. Series.
E807.1.R48S38   1995
973.917'092—dc20
    [B]   94-29329
                                         CIP
                                         AC

Printed in the United States of America

10 9 8 7 6 5 4 3 2 1

Illustration Credits:
Department of Tourism, New Brunswick, Canada, p. 48; Franklin Delano
Roosevelt Library, pp. 6, 15, 18, 22, 31, 38, 43, 46, 53, 62, 79, 80, 93,
106, 110, 112; Little White House State Historic Site, p. 82; Michael A.
Schuman, pp. 34, 58, 60; United Nations Photo 165054\Lois Conner, p.
86.

Cover Illustration:
Franklin Delano Roosevelt Library

Contents

Eleanor Roosevelt

1

Burning the Midnight Oil at the UN

Most of the residents in Paris, France, were sound asleep on December 10, 1948. They did not know that in a building called the Palais de Chaillot, in the center of the city, a group of people was making history. After all, it was just 3:00 A.M. But tired delegates to the third session of the United Nations (UN) General Assembly were voting to adopt a document. This document has been called one of the most important endorsements of human rights in the twentieth century.

Among the delegates was a tall gray-haired woman dressed in prim clothing and carrying a briefcase. She was Eleanor Roosevelt, former First Lady of the United States and chair of the UN Commission on Human Rights. One of her duties as chair was the drafting of a "Universal Declaration of Human Rights." Many observers felt that it would be very difficult—if not impossible—to compose such a document that would satisfy all the leaders of the various countries in the UN.

The UN was a brand-new body when Eleanor Roosevelt was named to the committee in 1945. She had a reputation for being concerned about people—especially the poor and powerless—and was a logical choice for such a job. Also Roosevelt wanted to prove to doubters that an organization such as the UN really could work. Many in the U.S. government had little faith in the ability of the world's nations to sit down and work out their problems. Roosevelt felt that the "Universal Declaration of Human Rights," in which all nations agreed that all people are entitled to basic liberties, would answer the pessimists.

The vote taken that December morning proved Roosevelt was right. A total of forty-eight nations voted in favor of the declaration, with eight abstaining and zero voting against it. Two nations' representatives were absent. After the vote was completed Roosevelt wrote "long job finished."[1]

The job truly was a long one. The first meeting of the UN Commission on Human Rights was held April 29, 1946. And over the two years of debate that followed there were many disagreements and squabbles among the member nations. Some disputes were over vital issues. To understand the times, it is important to know that the former Soviet Union, and its political allies, believed in communism—a different form of government than that of the United States.

The form of government in the United States is representative democracy, in which the country's citizens elect their leaders. The economic system in the United States is capitalism, in which manufacturing and services are privately owned and compete with each other for business. Those who believe in capitalism feel that workers will produce more when they are personally rewarded with incentives such as higher wages or bonuses.

In pure communism all manufacturing and services are owned by the community. There is no private ownership and no competition. Those who believe in communism feel that the citizens of a community will work together for the benefit of the community as a whole.

However, in the Soviet Union's variation of communism, the government owned all production and property and there was just one official political party—the Communist Party. Officially the country was atheistic, and citizens' actions were tightly controlled by the government. Those who believed in ideas contrary to those of the government were commonly jailed or exiled. The Soviet Union's leader at the time, Joseph Stalin, was a dictator. He ruled his country with an iron fist, and the communist countries in eastern Europe were really his puppets.

Other disagreements arose over simple issues such as words. But every word in a document like this is likely to be taken literally by government leaders. The original declaration read, "All men are created equal"—just as it reads in the American Declaration of Independence.

The delegate from India, a woman, said that people in her country might interpret this to mean that women were not to be included. Roosevelt responded by saying that American women have never felt left out because the Declaration of Independence reads "all men." But the Indian delegate said that in her country men would take the words literally. So the declaration draft was changed from "all men" to "all human beings."[2]

Roosevelt was a hard worker and she expected the same from her fellow delegates. She often held sessions well into the evenings and on weekends. Thus it was not unusual for committee members to complain about the long hours.

In her newspaper column called "My Day," which Roosevelt wrote for nearly thirty years, she commented about the committee's work. "Without any question, I've been almost a slave driver as the chairman," she said, "but one of the members came to me and said he felt that, on the whole, we'd accomplished more because we had set a date to finish our work and had stuck to it."[3]

When she was young, Eleanor Roosevelt seemed least likely to someday head such an important committee—or even to have any kind of public life at all. As a girl she was shy and insecure.[4] Her mother was disappointed that she was not pretty, and called her "Granny" since Eleanor tended to be old-fashioned in her ways.[5]

It is also hard to conceive that this woman, who supported both the rights of women and of African Americans, believed as a young adult "that men were superior creatures, and . . . knew more about politics than women."[6] As a young adult she also thought that African Americans, whom she and many other whites at the time called "darkies," were an inferior race, not even to be used as servants.[7]

As Roosevelt matured and became educated she gradually outgrew her ignorant opinions. By the time she was First Lady she received criticism from people who felt that she was too supportive of women, African Americans, Jews, and other minorities.

The "Universal Declaration of Human Rights" might be Eleanor Roosevelt's most lasting legacy. Russian dissident and Nobel Peace Prize winner Alexander Solzhenitsyn called it the "best document" ever produced by the UN.[8]

U Thant, a famous secretary-general of the UN, called it the "Magna Carta of mankind."[9] (The Magna Carta is an exceptional document that was signed by King John of England in 1215. It granted civil liberties to the English people, and was the first document of its kind.)

Many nations that later became independent in the 1960s and 1970s—including Cyprus, Jamaica, and several African countries—placed statements inspired by the "Universal Declaration of Human Rights" into their own constitutions. And numerous international conventions and peace treaties have included references to the declaration in legally binding statements.

To many, however, Eleanor Roosevelt is remembered not for any one accomplishment, but as a humanitarian who cared more for the world's citizens than for herself. Because of this image she became known as the "First Lady of the World."

2

A Lonely Childhood

An old saying warns that "money can't buy happiness." For Eleanor Roosevelt, this adage was true. Despite the fact that she was born into a family of wealth and privilege, Eleanor had an unhappy childhood, which some say affected her behavior throughout life.[1]

Anna Eleanor Roosevelt was born on October 14, 1884, into high society in New York City. High society meant that her family was upper class and distinguished in its community. She could also claim a long line of ancestors in America. Eleanor's ancestors on both her mother's and father's sides had been in the United States since the 1600s and both families had been prominent in New York.

It was not unusual for her family to sail to Europe for weeks at a stretch. Or the Roosevelts might spend leisure time at their second home, a country estate in the woods of Long Island. Then again they might visit their third home, called Tivoli. Tivoli was Eleanor's grandmother's home, located on the shore of the Hudson River.

When she was older Little Nell, as Eleanor was called by her father (she was never called by her given first name Anna), was educated at an exclusive private school in England. Her uncle, Theodore Roosevelt, would become President of the United States. Money and prestige were never problems for the Roosevelt family.

But with wealth came obligations. Those people born into high society in New York City were expected to set an example and share their time and money by helping in hospitals or giving donations to the poor. Little Nell could often be seen accompanying her father around town as he performed deeds of charity.

Eleanor said that because of her social status she also lost some of her free will. It was expected that she would socialize with the "right people," meaning those from the same ancestry and background as her own. When she was a girl in the late 1800s, it was viewed as improper for someone from her background to associate with the "common" (or poor) people unless she was performing an act of charity. Those who did not conform to these unwritten rules were looked upon in disgrace. Thus, Eleanor Roosevelt was raised in a very sheltered world.

But there were other factors that also affected her

Tivoli Mansion, on the shore of the Hudson River, was the country estate of Eleanor's family. It was the home of Eleanor's grandmother, Mary Livingston Hall.

childhood. Little Nell felt considerably closer to her father, who doted on her, than her mother.[2] Part of the reason why Elliott Roosevelt fussed so much over his daughter may have stemmed from two tragedies that befell him shortly before Eleanor's birth.

On February 14, 1884, both his mother—Martha Bulloch Roosevelt—and his sister-in-law—Theodore's wife Alice Lee Roosevelt—died within hours of each other. Alice died in childbirth shortly after delivering her baby daughter, also named Alice. His mother passed away as a result of typhoid fever, a disease usually caused by bad food or water.

In her autobiography Eleanor Roosevelt wrote, "My father felt these losses deeply. . . . Very soon, however, in October 1884, I came into the world, and from all accounts I must have been a more wrinkled and less attractive baby than the average—but to him I was a miracle from Heaven."[3]

That was not the only time Eleanor referred to herself as homely. As an adult she stood nearly six feet tall—quite large for a woman of her time. And as a child Eleanor compared herself to her mother Anna Hall Roosevelt. Anna was an extraordinarily beautiful woman, and beautiful women seemed to run in her family. In fact, the first sentence in Eleanor's autobiography is not about her, but about her mother. "My mother was one of the most beautiful women I have ever seen," she wrote.[4]

Eleanor believed that her mother looked down upon her because she lacked physical beauty. She said that her mother tried to teach her proper manners to compensate for her looks. That request only made Eleanor more self-conscious about her physical appearance.[5]

Eleanor even recalled how her mother called her "Granny," sometimes in front of other people. Regardless of whether her mother meant the nickname to be demeaning, Little Nell took it as an insult.[6]

In other ways Eleanor felt herself to be inadequate in the eyes of her parents. She recalled being exceedingly shy as a youngster, and her shyness embarrassed her mother. Once when called upon by her teacher to spell aloud some easy words, Eleanor remained quiet—too bashful to answer. In response her mother gave her a prompt scolding.

One of Eleanor's earliest memories took place when she was about two-and-a-half years old and was on board a steamship with her family, sailing to Europe. During their first day at sea the air was filled with fog. Due to the poor visibility, their ship was hit by another one, causing a dreadful accident and dozens of injuries.

As an adult Eleanor remembered incredible confusion at the time of the accident. Her father escaped into a lifeboat and a crew member on the ship held Eleanor by the arms, trying to ease her down to her anxious father. Eleanor shrieked and cried at first, refusing to let go. After several agonizing minutes she did

Anna Hall and Elliott Roosevelt, Eleanor's parents. Anna Hall
Roosevelt was an extraordinarily beautiful woman, and Eleanor
considered herself homely in comparison.

let go, and the whole family was taken safely back to New York.

Shortly afterward her parents tried making the trip again, but Eleanor was now so scared of ships, heights, and water that she refused to go along. So she was left behind to stay with a great aunt, whom she called Auntie Gracie, on Long Island until her parents returned. One can't help but wonder what effect the near-tragedy had on a little girl at such an impressionable age. Perhaps she thought it was her fault that she panicked and was left behind.[7]

A few years later, just before her sixth birthday, Eleanor did successfully sail to Europe with her parents. In Italy she was given a donkey along with a boy attendant for the donkey. With this arrangement she could ride on the roads alongside her family as the boy led the donkey. But when they approached a steep downgrade Eleanor became frightened and refused to descend. In response her father accused her of cowardice.

Eleanor wrote that while she always knew she was first in her father's heart, she said that he often became annoyed when she showed fear or a lack of courage. Is that what he felt when she panicked and refused to sail with her parents when they journeyed to Europe?

On the trip to Italy, Eleanor displayed the kind of concern for others that she would become known for as an adult. On one donkey ride she noticed that her attendant's feet were cut and bleeding. Thinking of his pain, she switched places with the poor boy and let him ride the donkey home while she ran alongside it.

Was Eleanor really the homely girl she thought herself? She hated her long legs, feeling they made her appear ungainly. Eleanor also felt that the dresses she wore were too short for her build and emphasized her awkwardness. (Short dresses would not become fashionable for decades.)

Not everyone agreed with Eleanor's assessment of herself. During her adult life Eleanor's cousin Alice was bitter toward Eleanor, and their feud was well known to the public. It was not unusual for Alice to publicly insult both Eleanor's character and looks. But in her later years Alice wrote about Eleanor's younger days. She said:

> [Eleanor] made a big thing about having long legs and having to wear short dresses. Well, as far as I was concerned, I envied her long legs and didn't notice her short skirts, if indeed they were short.[8]

Alice continued her appraisal of her young cousin, and the way she admired Eleanor from a distance:

> She was always making herself out to be an ugly duckling but she was really rather attractive. Tall, rather coltish-looking, with masses of pale, gold hair rippling to below her waist, and really lovely blue eyes. It's true that her chin went in a bit, which wouldn't have been so noticeable if only her hateful grandmother had fixed her teeth. I think that Eleanor today would have been considered a

beauty, not in the classical sense but as an attractive, rather unusual person in her own right.[9]

As Alice stated, it was Eleanor's grandmother, Mary Livingston Hall—not her parents—who had charge of Eleanor as an adolescent. For by the time Eleanor was ten, both her parents had died. Her grandmother would raise her and her younger brother, Gracie Hall Roosevelt, in both New York City and at her country retreat called Tivoli.

Eleanor's mother Anna died on December 7, 1892, from diphtheria. This disease, a highly contagious one at that time, caused blockage of the throat. Eleanor was eight and her mother was only twenty-seven. (Nowadays people are regularly vaccinated for diphtheria shortly after birth.)

Never close to her mother, Eleanor showed little sadness at her death. She later wrote in her autobiography, "Death meant nothing to me, and one fact wiped out everything else—my father was back and I would see him very soon."[10]

Elliott Roosevelt continued to bathe his daughter in gifts and love. He arranged for her to have the best teachers and bought her a pony so that she could learn to become a good horsewoman. But tragically he would die less than two years after Eleanor's mother.

It is likely that Elliott Roosevelt suffered from mental depression and alcoholism, but in his day little was known about mental illness. He was hospitalized several

Eleanor (far right) poses with her two brothers, Elliott and Gracie Hall, and her father, Elliott Roosevelt, in 1892.

times for treatment, though little progress was accomplished.[11]

Today these two conditions are controllable with medication and counseling. There are also support groups today for people with problems such as alcohol addiction. But in the late 1800s it was all too common to treat depression and other mental illnesses with alcohol. This strategy only made someone like Eleanor's father more dependent on the substance. Elliott Roosevelt died from complications of alcoholism on August 14, 1894.

Eleanor later wrote, "I simply refused to believe it and went to bed weeping, I finally went to sleep and began the next day living in my dream world as usual. My grandmother decided that we children should not go to the funeral, and so I had no tangible thing to make death real to me."[12]

3

Gaining Self-Confidence

Despite what cousin Alice said, Eleanor Roosevelt's grandmother Mary Hall was not really "hateful." She was just very strict and old-fashioned—even for her day. But she was truly concerned about Eleanor's well-being. She insisted that Eleanor wear very warm clothes from the first day of November through the first day of April, in spite of whether it was warm or cold outside.

And there was a set of rules just for Sundays, when no game playing or leisure reading was allowed. Instead, Eleanor was to spend the day teaching hymns and religious studies to the coachman's small daughter, then recite the same to her grandmother.

Eleanor lived with Mary Hall until she was fifteen. During these years she helped with household chores. She also read a great deal (although Sunday reading was limited to religious texts). Some of her leisure time was spent at Sagamore Hill, the Long Island home of her "Uncle Ted," the future President Theodore Roosevelt. Most of her time at Sagamore Hill was devoted to family outings, at which the Roosevelts picnicked and camped.

There were also obligatory Christmas parties and dances when Eleanor was in her early teens. Since she saw herself as clumsy and homely, Eleanor found the parties to be painful. She later said:

> I was a poor dancer, and the climax of the party was a dance. I still remember the inappropriate dresses I wore—and, worst of all—they were above my knees. I knew, of course, I was different from all the other girls and if I had not known, they were frantic in telling me so! I still remember my gratitude at one of these parties to my cousin Franklin Roosevelt when he came and asked me to dance with him![1]

Eleanor would meet her distant cousin Franklin again in a few years. But first there were other plans. Eleanor's mother had wanted her to be educated in Europe, and her grandmother remembered that.

So at age fifteen Eleanor sailed to England with her "Aunt Tissie." There she attended a private boarding school for girls, called Allenswood, located outside London.

Allenswood was a progressive school run by a French headmistress named Marie Souvestre. Eleanor would later say that she was one of the most influential persons in her life. Mademoiselle Souvestre was short and stocky, with a head full of white hair pulled straight back. She was a very open-minded person for her day, believing in pacifism and feminism. Unlike Eleanor's mother and grandmother, she inspired Eleanor to ask questions and challenge conventional thinking.[2]

The headmistress took an immediate liking to Eleanor and helped the teenager gain self-confidence. She urged Eleanor to discard her dowdy outfits and use her allowance to buy more fashionable and flattering clothes. Eleanor did so and wore them proudly. Mademoiselle Souvestre also recognized Eleanor's natural abilities for writing and conversing, and she helped Eleanor perfect these skills.

Soon after Eleanor arrived at Allenswood, Mademoiselle Souvestre wrote to Eleanor's grandmother. She said that the girl showed a "purity of her heart" and "nobleness of her thought." Souvestre added, "I have not found her easily influenced in anything that was not straightforward and honest."[3]

During the three years Eleanor attended Allenswood, she was among Mademoiselle Souvestre's favorite students. She was chosen to sit opposite the headmistress at dinner, a place of honor. Eleanor recalled that the special position had many benefits; it allowed her to learn a lot, sample special dishes at formal dinners, and even overhear a bit of gossip now and then.

If Eleanor was a "teacher's pet," her classmates were

neither resentful nor jealous. Eleanor's cousin Corinne, who also attended Allenswood, said that Eleanor was Mademoiselle Souvestre's "supreme favorite and what was remarkable was that she had made no enemies through this favoritism."[4] Perhaps it was Eleanor's natural humility and concern for others that showed through, causing her classmates to harbor no ill feelings toward her.

During school breaks Mademoiselle Souvestre offered to take Eleanor on trips through Europe with her. At various times they traveled together to different cities and regions of France and Italy. Eleanor later wrote that Souvestre taught her how to enjoy visiting different places in several ways. One was stressing a relaxed form of travel. Another was eating local cuisine. A third way was seeking out settings where one would meet natives and not other tourists. "Never again would I be the rigid little person I had been theretofore," Eleanor later wrote about this period.[5]

Modern in her attitudes, Mademoiselle Souvestre also permitted Eleanor to go sightseeing on her own in Europe with no chaperone. At that time it was not considered proper for a young girl to travel alone. By coincidence Eleanor unexpectedly met some neighbors from New York while sightseeing in Paris. They wrote to Eleanor's grandmother, who demanded that Eleanor return home immediately.

Eleanor hated the idea of going home, and

Mademoiselle Souvestre was regretful about losing her favorite student. But Eleanor felt it would not be right to disobey her grandmother's wishes. So home she went for the summer, not expecting to return to Allenswood.

Mademoiselle Souvestre wrote a letter to Eleanor's grandmother, expressing her disappointment. She wrote, "Eleanor has had the most admirable influence on the school and gained the affection of many and the respect of all. To me personally I feel I lose a dear friend in her."[6]

That summer was an unhappy one. Eleanor spent it with her family in the resort town of Northeast Harbor, Maine. However, she felt uncomfortable around the people there. She also had a very hurtful conversation with her Auntie Corinne. Frustrated with her own social life, Auntie Corinne called Eleanor the "ugly duckling" of the family, and told her she would never have a boyfriend. She also told Eleanor some details of her father's condition in his last days, which Eleanor had never heard before. It was devastating for Eleanor to hear unkind words about her beloved father.[7]

These unpleasant experiences made Eleanor more determined than ever to return to Allenswood for her final year. After much persuasion her grandmother agreed. Eleanor enjoyed her last year as much as the previous two, and again spent much time traveling through Europe with Mademoiselle Souvestre. Eleanor would keep in touch with Mademoiselle Souvestre for several years after leaving Europe, until her best friend and mentor died of cancer on March 30, 1905. That was just a few months before Eleanor would revisit Allenswood during her honeymoon.

Upon returning home, Eleanor saw her distant cousin Franklin Delano Roosevelt at several coming out parties. These parties were a series of formal gatherings and dances accompanying a woman's eighteenth birthday and were part of the customs of high society. Eleanor hated the parties, finding them uncomfortable and nerve-racking. She enjoyed much more the hours she spent volunteering in the slums of New York City.[8]

As a member of a group called the Consumers' League, she investigated working conditions in factories informally called "sweatshops." Here poor people worked in deplorable conditions. Upon finding problems, such as dirty sanitary facilities or unsatisfactory lighting, she lobbied government authorities for improvements.

But Eleanor's favorite volunteer work was teaching exercise and dance to young girls in New York's impoverished Lower East Side in a center for social reform called the College Settlement. (This preference was in spite of the fact that she belittled her own dancing ability.)

There were few child labor laws at the time, and it was common for young children to work twelve hours or more a day in filthy, noisy, dark factories. Eleanor was truly impressed with the children she met and wrote to Franklin that her work with them was "the nicest part of my day."[9]

Fearing for her health and safety, members of her family disliked Eleanor spending so much time working with the poor. One cousin begged her to quit volunteer work and spend the summer resting and relaxing in the leisure town of Newport, Rhode Island. But Eleanor ignored her family's pleas. She truly enjoyed making a difference in people's lives. Besides, her work with poor children reminded her of the similar good deeds that she had done with her father when she was a child.

One person who encouraged her to continue her volunteer work was Franklin. He was greatly impressed by her willingness to give her time and effort to help others. Eleanor and Franklin would meet after her classes at College Settlement. Later she visited him while he was attending Harvard University in Cambridge, Massachusetts.

Though she thought herself awkward and homely, and was even told so by relatives such as her Aunt Corinne, Eleanor as a young woman did not lack boyfriends. Her aunt's prediction that Eleanor would never have a boyfriend was completely wrong.

A trio of wealthy and eligible young men from her social background—Nicholas Biddle, Lyman Delano, and Howard Cary—were among several who admired her. But Eleanor was falling in love with Franklin, and

Eleanor and Franklin Delano Roosevelt, on their honeymoon trip to Europe in 1905.

they became secretly engaged in 1903. They publicly announced their engagement on December 1, 1904.

Upon his engagement Franklin wrote to his mother Sara Delano Roosevelt:

> I am the happiest man just now in the world; likewise the luckiest—And for you dear Mummy, you know nothing can ever change what we have always been & always will be to each other—and only now you have two children to love & to love you—and Eleanor as you know will always be a daughter to you in every true way. . . .[10]

On March 17, 1905 (Saint Patrick's Day), Franklin and Eleanor were married in a cousin's home in New York City. Eleanor's Uncle Ted, then President of the United States, gave away the bride. The presence of the President created some inconvenience, such as heavy security, that caused a few invited guests to miss the ceremony.

In fact, Eleanor laughingly said that immediately after the ceremony most guests seemed more interested in seeing and hearing the President than being with her and her husband. As their guests followed Eleanor's Uncle Ted into the library where refreshments were being served, the bride and groom were left standing alone. She later wrote, "We simply followed the crowd and listened with the rest."[11]

4

A Politician's Wife

In a way Franklin got his wish; Eleanor Roosevelt did become like a daughter to her mother-in-law, but it was to the extent that she was completely dominated by Sara. Eleanor and Franklin returned from a belated honeymoon trip in Europe to discover that Sara Roosevelt had already purchased the young couple a house three blocks from her own in New York City. Franklin's mother also furnished the house to her own liking. She filled it with servants without even checking with her son and new daughter-in-law.

In addition Sara Roosevelt ruled her country retreat in Hyde Park, north of New York City. This is where Franklin was born and where the couple would also spend much time. Growing up as she did in her grandmother's house, Eleanor had always wanted a

Sara Roosevelt's country retreat in Hyde Park, New York was the birthplace of Franklin Roosevelt. The couple would spend much time in this home.

home of her own. Yet lacking a traditional upbringing with her own parents, she also had an urge to be loved. She wrote to her mother-in-law after her marriage, "I do so want you to learn to love me a little. You must know that I will always try to do what you wish. . . ."[1]

Her aching urge to be loved was stronger than the wish for her own home, so Eleanor fell into place as an obedient daughter-in-law. Pressured by her mother-in-law's strong personality and wanting so much to please, she gave in to Sara's every whim and desire. When the Roosevelts' first baby—a daughter named Anna Eleanor for her mother—was born in 1906, Sara would not let Eleanor raise the girl on her own. Instead Sara and a staff of servants and nurses, many cold and impersonal, did most of the child rearing. Eleanor later said it was a mistake to let servants raise her children.[2]

In December 1907, Eleanor gave birth to a boy James, named for Franklin's father. A year later her mother-in-law built two attached houses in another part of the city for herself, Franklin, and Eleanor to live in. Sliding doors between the houses gave Sara the capability to enter Eleanor and Franklin's private space whenever she chose.

A few weeks after moving into their new house, Franklin found Eleanor sitting and crying at her dressing table. He asked what was the matter and she told him how uncomfortable she felt living in a house where she could not feel at home. He seemed unconcerned and told her that she would feel better in a little while. Afterward she blamed herself "for acting like a little fool."[3]

It wasn't until 1910—when Franklin was elected to the state legislature in Albany, New York—that Eleanor Roosevelt was able to break from the tight reins of her mother-in-law.

Because of her sheltered background, Eleanor knew little of how politics worked. And despite the fact that today she is revered as an early champion of women's rights, at the age of twenty-six in 1910, she believed men were generally superior to and better suited for politics than women. She also wrote, "It was a wife's duty to be interested in whatever interested her husband, whether it was politics, books, or a particular dish for dinner."[4]

While her husband entertained fellow legislators at home, Eleanor chatted with politicians' wives about the weather or other neutral topics. On late nights when the maid had gone to sleep, Eleanor would bring snacks of beer, cheese, and crackers to the men.

But she also attended legislative debates and spoke with her husband's constituents (the persons living in the district he represented). She took the initiative to study the issues, educating herself on the workings of politics. She got to know politicians and newspaper reporters and enjoyed talking with them—much more than with the socialites back in New York City. In time she saw firsthand both the good and bad sides of political life.

At the same time Eleanor was learning about political workings, Franklin and Eleanor were enlarging their family. From 1906 through 1910 Eleanor was almost always pregnant. By 1910 she had given birth to four children—three boys and a girl, but one son died very young.

After Anna and James, a third baby was a boy named Franklin, Jr. He was born in 1909, but died when just seven months old from a viral disease called influenza. Eleanor was heartbroken, and like many people in similar circumstances, she blamed herself. She felt that she had been inadequate as a mother to the baby.[5]

Another son, Elliott, was born the next year. He was a very excitable baby, and Eleanor blamed herself for his disposition. She felt that the boy's disposition was a result of her moodiness when she was pregnant with him so soon after Franklin, Jr.'s death. She knew from her childhood tragedies that such things happen in life, and gradually, she learned to accept the sadness of the baby's death.[6]

In Albany, Eleanor was able to become more involved with her children. Without nurses, maids, servants, or a strong-willed mother-in-law to command her life, she was able to spend much time with the young ones. She read to them, held children's teas before dinner, and played with them afterward.

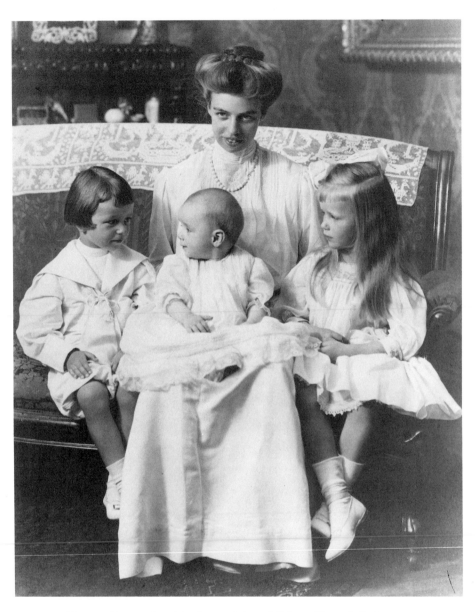

Eleanor Roosevelt with three of her children (from left) James, Elliott, and Anna. Roosevelt was very involved with her children during the family's time in Albany, New York.

The Roosevelts did not stay in Albany long. In 1912 Woodrow Wilson was elected the 27th President of the United States, and Franklin was chosen to be Assistant Secretary of the Navy. This job was the same one Eleanor's Uncle Ted held before he became President. Franklin and Eleanor were soon on their way to Washington, D.C.

For the first few years Eleanor fulfilled her duties as a political wife. She attended functions, hosted parties, and met with other political wives. In 1914 when war broke out in Europe, Eleanor publicly supported her husband's stand. Franklin believed that the United States must be better prepared militarily than it was and that the size of the Navy should be increased. Privately, however, she was sympathetic to the anti-war philosophies of politicians such as William Jennings Bryan and activists such as Jane Addams.[7]

She also gave birth to another son in 1914. The Roosevelts named him Franklin, Jr., in memory of the baby who died. Another boy was born in 1916. He was named John and would be the last of Franklin and Eleanor's children.

Here in Washington, Eleanor continued her dual roles as politician's wife and mother. She felt education for her children was vital. It was her belief that a child's early years were most important and that learning at home was necessary for any success at school.[8]

Like most mothers she worried greatly about her

children, especially when she and Franklin had to be away from home. One time when daughter Anna was about seven, she anxiously asked her mother—who was about to depart on a trip—what would happen if the children had to buy anything "or got lost or put into prison."[9] Needless to say, the children never were put into prison and everything turned out all right.

Once in a while, however, there was an accident. Franklin's family had a summer home on Campobello Island in New Brunswick, Canada. One summer on Campobello, while the youngsters were in the care of their nurse—the children made a small fire on the beach. When the nurse turned her back, little Elliott fell onto some hot ashes and burned his arms and legs. Eleanor wrote to Franklin—who was away on a political trip—saying that Elliott "only cried a little & Nurse says they are only skin burns."[10] Medicinal cream was placed on his burns and Elliott recovered with no major problems.

When the United States entered the war—later to be called World War I—on April 6, 1917, Eleanor Roosevelt, like other political wives, did her part. She organized and actively worked in the local Red Cross Canteen. On one occasion she sliced her finger almost to the bone while operating a bread cutting machine. The day had been incredibly busy, and Eleanor continued working at her shift for hours before getting medical attention. She carried the scar from this wound for the rest of her life.

Eleanor also knitted woolen garments to be donated to the Navy League and visited wounded and shell-shocked Navy men in Washington, D.C., hospitals. At one of these hospitals she exhibited her social conscience and natural instinct to right any wrongs.

She would drive the grounds of the naval unit of Saint Elizabeth's Hospital, where shell-shocked veterans were receiving mental health treatment for stress caused by war experiences. Here she observed patients in various states of neglect. Some stared blankly into space or paced back and forth; few received sufficient treatment.

Eleanor immediately contacted the Secretary of the Department of the Interior, under whose jurisdiction the hospital was. She told him what she had seen. The secretary investigated and organized a committee to appear before Congress to ask that more money be spent on the hospital. The request was granted, and conditions were greatly improved.

On another occasion she felt a recreation center for wounded war veterans was needed to aid the men in their occupational therapy treatments. So she took the initiative to ask an organization called the Colonial Dames, a patriotic women's society dedicated to the preservation of colonial buildings and relics, for funding. They complied, and the center was built.

Politics can often split families and ruin friendships, but Eleanor Roosevelt had a way of appealing to the better nature in people. Her Uncle Ted, the former

President, wanted to organize a division of men to fight in the European war. However President Wilson rejected his request. Uncle Ted, a Republican, was disappointed that Wilson, a Democrat, refused him. As much as Eleanor hated to see her uncle upset, she stayed loyal to Wilson in her husband's interest. Her uncle never held this action against her, and she stayed on good terms with him until he died in 1919.

Unfortunately family relationships would not remain so amiable in 1920, when Franklin was nominated for Vice-President of the United States. The candidate running for President was Ohio governor James M. Cox, a dark horse and compromise candidate nominated on the 44th ballot at the Democratic convention. Cox was not a strong supporter of President Wilson's policies. In order to balance the ticket, it was felt that a Wilson loyalist should be nominated for Vice President. So Franklin Roosevelt got the nod.

Of course, Eleanor actively supported her husband. In September she joined him and his staff on a four-week-long campaign trip that went by train from New York to Colorado. She was the only woman on the train among all the newspaper reporters and campaign aides. In the beginning she felt bored and uneasy.

Gradually she began feeling more comfortable. One of Franklin's closest aides, a man named Louis Howe, tried his best to put Eleanor at ease. He occasionally asked her opinion on a speech her husband was about to

Louis Howe, one of Franklin Roosevelt's closest aides, helped
Eleanor Roosevelt adapt to being a candidate's wife. The two
became good friends.

give. In time Howe and Eleanor became best friends, and he helped her adjust to the unselected job of being a candidate's wife. One time he even took her sightseeing to Niagara Falls, New York, while Franklin was in a nearby town giving a speech Eleanor had heard many times over. Mostly, though, she appeared alongside her husband, showing her unconditional support.

Eleanor's Republican relatives and in-laws resented her joining the opposition. They publicly blasted both her and Franklin. Eleanor's first cousin—Theodore Roosevelt, Jr.—followed Franklin to communities where he had just spoken. The former President's son stressed to voters how much his side of the family differed from the Democratic vice-presidential candidate. He stated that the Republican Roosevelts were the true Roosevelts. Uncle Ted's widow Edith resorted to name calling, as did cousin Alice.[11]

Alice had been critical of Eleanor for some time by now, and Eleanor usually brushed aside her cousin's attitude. But Eleanor found the accusation of being a traitor to her family very hard to overlook.[12] What had been simple bickering between Eleanor and Alice had hardened into a real feud. This feud would continue for the rest of their lives.

Some observers believed that Alice was jealous of Eleanor because Alice's father, Theodore Roosevelt, actually had more in common with Eleanor than with his own daughter. Many thought Alice, nicknamed

"Princess Alice" by the press, was jealous because she had wanted to marry Franklin.

Alice denied such talk as foolishness. "Nothing could be further from the truth. I don't think it crossed either of our minds for a moment," she said.[13] She was married in a White House wedding in 1906 to Ohio Congressperson Nicholas Longworth.

As events turned out, Cox and Roosevelt lost the election in a landslide to Republicans Warren G. Harding and Calvin Coolidge. Eleanor explained that Franklin was not surprised by the defeat, and in fact, had expected it and accepted it matter-of-factly.[14]

On the outside the Roosevelt marriage seemed to be a happy one, but there were problems that the general public could not have known about. Unlike Franklin's casual acceptance of his political defeat, this matter was something Eleanor would not take so passively.

In September 1918, Franklin was sick with pneumonia and Eleanor was taking care of his mail. While doing so she came across private love letters written between Franklin and Eleanor's social secretary Lucy Mercer. It was obvious that Franklin and Lucy, who was seven years younger than Eleanor, were in love and had been having an affair for years. Eleanor offered Franklin a divorce, but his mother, Sara insisted on saving the marriage. And Franklin was aware that a divorce would ruin his political career. Franklin agreed never to see Lucy again.[15]

Alice Roosevelt Longworth, Eleanor Roosevelt's cousin, was nicknamed "Princess Alice" by the press. She is shown here in 1902.

However, this incident gave Eleanor one more reason to feel insecure about herself. Cousin Alice, meanwhile, encouraged the affair, claiming that it was good for Franklin. She said, "He deserved a good time. He was married to Eleanor."[16]

Following his 1920 political defeat, Franklin went to work in private business as vice-president of a banking firm in New York City. Eleanor and Franklin moved back to the same home they earlier shared with Sara.

On August 10, 1921, while at Campobello, Franklin took a swim in a warm lake before diving in to the chilly waters of the Bay of Fundy. He could not have known that both his and Eleanor's lives would be forever different from that day on.

As he returned to the house from the swim, Franklin began to feel weary. He later recalled, "When I reached the house, the mail was in with several newspapers I hadn't seen. I sat reading for a while, too tired even to dress."[17]

After reading for a few hours he began to feel chilled. Skipping dinner, Franklin went to bed. He slept poorly and awoke the next morning with a fever. While climbing out of bed he had trouble moving his left leg, and before the day was over, he had lost complete movement in both legs.

Two doctors were called, but they misdiagnosed Franklin's ailment. One prescribed massage, and for two

The Roosevelts' house on Campobello Island. The family spent leisure time at this summer retreat in New Brunswick, Canada.

weeks Eleanor and Louis Howe followed this doctor's advice. But the pain in Franklin's legs only increased.

Finally an orthopedics specialist was called. He diagnosed the condition as poliomyelitis, or polio. Polio can be avoided today by a vaccine, but there was no vaccine in 1921. The vigorous massage had only made the affliction worse. Franklin Roosevelt would never walk again without the aid of crutches, and he would spend most of his waking hours in a wheelchair.

5

Franklin's Eyes and Hands

In the second volume of her autobiography Eleanor wrote about her husband's polio. She said:

> People have often asked me how I myself felt about his illness. To tell the truth, I do not think I ever stopped to analyze my feelings. There was so much to do to manage the household and the children and to try to keep things running smoothly that I never had any time to think of my own reactions. I simply lived from day to day and got through the best I could.[1]

Eleanor might not have consciously thought about her feelings after Franklin was stricken with polio. But history shows that she reacted with strength and determination. She did confess years later that "his illness finally made me stand on my own two feet. . . ."[2]

Now that Franklin was physically unable to play

actively with the children, Eleanor took over what had been his established role. She was still fearful of swimming, a likely legacy of the terrifying experience she had as a toddler during the steamship accident. But she went with two political friends, Marion Dickerman and Nancy Cook, to take swimming lessons at the YWCA (Young Women's Christian Association).

She also learned to drive a car, since it was now necessary that she become more mobile. Learning to drive wasn't easy; she had two accidents early on, but ultimately gained self-confidence and became a competent driver. Believing that young boys should lead vigorous lives, she along with Dickerman and Cook took her two youngest sons and two other boys on a camping vacation. This had traditionally been a man's role. Eleanor and her friends had a fun time tent camping through New York's Adirondack Mountains, eastern Canada, and New Hampshire's White Mountains. They ended the trip at Campobello Island.

It was Eleanor's activity that spurred Franklin's political career. Sara Roosevelt wanted her son to retire from public service and settle down at the Hyde Park mansion to live a life of leisure. Both Eleanor and Louis Howe disagreed, however. They believed Franklin's doctor, who said a life of activity would be more beneficial to someone in Franklin's condition. Franklin also agreed.[3]

So Howe urged Eleanor to become more involved

with state Democratic politics, which would both keep Franklin interested in public life and the Roosevelt name in the public eye. She worked with the Women's Division of the Democratic State Committee of New York and eventually became finance chair, in charge of raising funds.

Thanks to female friends such as Dickerman and Cook, she also became politically involved in activist groups. Many, such as the League of Women Voters and the Women's Trade Union League, concerned women's rights. At first Eleanor was nervous and uncomfortable about speaking in public. But with Louis Howe's personal coaching, she became more and more at ease talking in front of groups.[4]

In her activist work she advocated liberal points of view for the time. These views included the eight-hour workday, child-labor laws, unemployment insurance, better public playgrounds and parks, school lunches, and the right of women to serve on juries. Many people opposed these ideas, and some even suggested Eleanor Roosevelt and her friends were anti-American for promoting them. Today these ideas are part of everyday life.

Many conservatives were also angered by her part on the Bok Peace Award committee. A magazine publisher named Edward Bok offered a prize of $50,000 (the equivalent of over $1 million today) to any person or group who developed the best workable plan for world

Eleanor Roosevelt (second from left) with her friends, including Marion Dickerman (far left) and Nancy Cook (second from right), in 1926. Thanks to them, she became involved in activist groups.

peace. A journalist and teacher named Esther Lape was given the job of administering the competition. Lape immediately asked Eleanor and another woman to work with her.

The judging committee consisted of both Democrats and Republicans, judges, university deans, editors, and military officers, including at least one general. Over 22,000 plans were received in all shapes and forms, including one outlawing war.

Even Franklin Roosevelt drew up a plan, although he did not submit it because his wife was on the administrative committee. His plan's premise was similar to that of the League of Nations—a forerunner of today's UN that was founded in the 1920s, but which the United States never joined. Franklin later considered the plan during his presidency when working on a charter for the UN.

The winning plan was submitted by a professor named Charles E. Levermore, who suggested a system of cooperation among nations. However, many hard-line conservatives—including those in both the media and the U.S. Senate—said the committee was anti-American. Known as isolationists, they believed that involvement in international affairs was contrary to the interests of the United States.

They charged that Bok, Lape, Eleanor, and the Bok Peace Award were the tools of "foreign governments and foreign institutions," and that the award "encouraged 'foreign entanglements' and 'communistic internationalism.'"[5]

The U.S. Senate Special Committee on Propaganda held hearings to decide whether the award and the committee were un-American. They concluded that both were, and the Bok committee was punished by losing its tax-exempt status. It was also reclassified as a "political lobby" rather than an "educational" group. Eleanor Roosevelt's name was placed in FBI (Federal Bureau of Investigation) files as being part of this un-American committee.

There is an ironic twist to this incident. Ten years later Frank B. Kellogg, secretary of state during the conservative Calvin Coolidge Administration, won the Nobel Peace Prize. He won it for negotiating the Kellogg-Briand Pact, a formal agreement aimed at outlawing war.

Despite the accusations and condemnations, Eleanor continued supporting the issues that were important to her. Thanks to her leadership, women were given much greater representation in the state Democratic party. In 1924 she was named chair of the women's platform committee, part of the Democratic National Committee. She said in one speech:

> It is disagreeable to take stands. It was always easier
> to compromise, always easier to let things go. To
> many women, and I am one of them, it is
> extraordinarily difficult to care about anything

enough to cause disagreement or unpleasant
feelings, but I have come to the conclusion that
this must be done for a time until we can prove
our strength and demand respect for our wishes. . . .
We will be enormously strengthened if we can
show that we are willing to fight to the very last
ditch for what we believe in.[6]

But at the national convention in New York, she was
disappointed to find that her group's ideas were basically
ignored by the men in power.[7] The highlight of the
convention was actually a standout performance by her
husband. In Franklin's first major public appearance
since contracting polio, he stood with the aid of only one
crutch. He was helped by his eldest son, James, who was
now sixteen years old. Roosevelt gave a rousing speech
nominating New York Governor Al Smith for President
of the United States. The speech was regarded as the
highlight of the convention, the crowd cheered loud and
strong for both his words and his courage. Franklin's
career had been rejuvenated.

The Democrats lost the 1924 general election to
Calvin Coolidge. Al Smith was, instead, re-elected
governor of New York. Eleanor spent the next few years
continuing to champion her causes, but she also did her
part to help the community of Hyde Park. Along with
Cook, Dickerman, and another mutual friend named
Caroline O'Day, Eleanor began a business called
Val-Kill Industries. It was named after Val-Kill Pond,
which bordered the Roosevelt's Hyde Park property.

The land had been owned by Franklin and was given to Eleanor and her friends to use as a retreat in 1924. The women arranged to have a little stone cottage built there in 1925 and the business began the next year.

In the 1920s more and more Americans were moving from the country to the city. Earning a living by agriculture, usually the only major business in rural regions, had become hard. The 1920 national census was the first in the nation's history to report a majority of Americans living in urban areas.

Hyde Park and the vicinity were no exception to this trend. Concerned by the migration of rural New Yorkers to urban areas, the four women decided that if farm workers were taught other skills that they could use to earn a living, they might not leave their homes.

A large, rambling, stucco building was constructed on the grounds of their retreat. Inside local workers made early American-style wooden furniture and other crafts. Val-Kill Industries was a success for ten years until it went out of business in 1936—one of many casualties of the Great Depression.

The business aside, the retreat gave Eleanor breathing room; a place where she could live away from the domination of her mother-in-law. Although she was forty years old, Eleanor was still forced by Sara Roosevelt to ask permission to bring friends to the Hyde Park mansion.

With her own retreat this was no longer necessary. She and her friends were in control. It was as if Eleanor

Val-Kill Industries was housed in this building on the land adjacent to the Roosevelts' Hyde Park property. Eleanor Roosevelt saw the place as a retreat from her mother-in-law's domineering influence.

now had a home of her own, something she never had before. After Franklin's death, she converted the defunct furniture factory into a home and lived there until her death seventeen years later. Val-Kill is open to the public as an historic home and looks as it did when she died. Visitors can see furniture made in the factory that was used by Eleanor Roosevelt in her home.

In addition to running Val-Kill, working for the Democratic party, advocating social change, and promoting charitable causes, Eleanor fulfilled a personal goal in 1927 by becoming a teacher. She, Dickerman, Cook, and O'Day purchased the Todhunter School for Girls in New York City. Dickerman, who had been vice-principal of the school, became principal.

Todhunter was very similar to Allenswood, the school Eleanor had attended in London. It was private and attracted mainly wealthy and privileged girls living in Manhattan. One of Todhunter's goals was to prepare its students for college in a time when not many women went on to higher education.

Roosevelt based her teaching on that of Marie Souvestre, employing a progressive yet informal and personal style. She tried to stimulate her students' minds by examining controversial topics. But she also held them personally accountable for their actions.

Like her former teacher, Roosevelt was greatly admired by her students. The feeling was mutual since she loved both teaching and young people. Roosevelt's

After her husband's death, Eleanor Roosevelt converted the Val-Kill factory into a home. Shown here is the living room, as it has been preserved.

message to her students was simple: Be somebody; Be yourself; Be all you can be.[8]

The subjects she taught included English and American literature, American history, and public affairs. She believed that public affairs courses might be more practical than other standard courses. To expose her charges to the lives of others less fortunate she took her students on trips to New York City's children's courts and tenements.

Even after her husband was elected governor of New York in 1928 and the Roosevelts moved to Albany, Eleanor refused to quit her teaching job. She commuted by train from Albany to New York City. She left home on Sunday evenings, returned to the governor's mansion on Wednesday evenings, and spent her time on the train grading homework and preparing lessons. The schedule was exhausting, but it gave her the opportunity to accomplish something on her own.

The 1928 presidential campaign was a disaster nationally for the Democrats, but a triumph locally. The presidential candidate, former New York governor Al Smith, was beaten in a landslide by sitting President Coolidge's Secretary of Commerce Herbert Hoover. Despite the national Republican victory, Franklin Roosevelt was elected governor of New York by a slim margin.

After the election Eleanor made a surprising statement to a reporter who asked how she felt about her husband's win. "If the rest of the ticket didn't get in,

Franklin and Eleanor Roosevelt relax with Franklin Roosevelt's secretary, Missy LeHand (center), at Val-Kill in 1930. That year, Franklin Delano Roosevelt was re-elected governor by a large margin.

what does it matter? . . . No I am not excited about my husband's election. I don't care. What difference can it make to me?"[9]

Later she explained to a friend that she was disappointed since the President can do much more for the country than a governor. But her frustration did not stop her from going above and beyond the standard expectations of a governor's wife. She went along with Franklin on his inspections of public institutions such as prisons, asylums, and hospitals. Since it was difficult for Franklin to walk inside the buildings, she served as his eyes and legs. In doing so, she not only helped the state, but learned a lot.

She recalled that her first reports were lacking:

> I would tell [Franklin] what was on the menu for the day and he would ask: 'Did you look to see whether the inmates actually were getting that food?' I learned to look into the cooking pots on the stove and find out if the contents corresponded to the menu; I learned to notice whether the beds were too close together, and whether they were folded up and put in closets or behind doors during the day, which would indicate that they filled the corridors at night . . . and before the end of our years in Albany, I had become a fairly expert reporter on state institutions.[10]

In 1930 Franklin was elected governor by a larger margin than in 1928, but in 1932 he did not run for governor. Bigger plans were in the works.

6

First Lady

By 1932, when Franklin's second term as governor was ending, the United States and much of the world was in the midst of a severe economic downturn known today as the Great Depression. Over twelve million Americans, or about 10 percent of the population, were out of work. The mood of the country was one of deep despair and hopelessness.[1]

What caused the Great Depression? Several factors have been attributed to it. The 1920s were a time of business prosperity and optimism. Many believe that Americans at the time acted as if the financial good fortune was endless and neglected to plan for the future. On October 29, 1929, the stock market "crashed," rendering the value of many stocks virtually worthless.

This event is regarded by most as the beginning of the Depression.

While the stock market crash might have been the most dramatic occurrence at the beginning of the Depression, the economy started to weaken months before October 1929. Two reasons for this included a glut of consumer goods and the unfair distribution of wealth, which made many Americans unable to buy these goods. Other reasons were faulty banking practices, the inability of farmers to export surpluses abroad because of high tariffs, and—perhaps the most given reason—excessive stock speculation.

President Hoover did exercise a limited amount of presidential initiative in responding to the hard times. But after three years of almost no economic improvement, American voters wanted a change in leadership. Franklin Roosevelt was nominated as the Democratic party's candidate for President of the United States. In November he overwhelmingly defeated President Hoover.

Franklin immediately drew up a plan of action for restoring the country's economic health. It consisted of creating broad social programs and government agencies, including funding public works. His plan was collectively known as The New Deal and had three main objectives. One aim was relief for both the unemployed and the farmers. The second aim was recovery of the economy, including some regulation of business. And the third aim was reform of the banking system. Although figures showed that improvement was slow, the New Deal was very popular with the American public.

But Eleanor, while happy for her husband and the Democratic party, was not pleased about her new role. "I never wanted to be a President's wife, and don't want it now," she told a reporter and friend named Lorena Hickok shortly after the election.[2]

She did not want to give up her activist work in order to become an official hostess for her husband, the traditional role of the First Lady. But Eleanor did fulfill the expected duties of the First Lady. She presided over receptions, state dinners, and teas for women's groups. But she refused to stop with this role, instead continuing her own career and becoming involved in the country's public policies.

Newspaper columnist Heywood Brown wrote at the time that he was "delighted to know that we are going to have a woman in the White House who feels . . . [that] she is before all else a human being and that she has a right to her own individual career regardless of the prominence of her husband."[3]

Roosevelt's concern for others continued to motivate her actions. In 1932 when Herbert Hoover was still President, veterans of World War I marched on Washington, D.C. They camped out in crude huts on the outskirts of town and demanded their bonus payments, even though it was several years before they were to receive the payments. The severity of the Depression had made the veterans, like many people, desperate.

President Hoover wanted the veterans peaceably evicted by the U.S. Army, the same Army that so many had fought with fifteen years earlier. But under General Douglas MacArthur the Army took violent action. The evacuation was a scene of pandemonium as the veterans rushed out of town while their huts were burned to the ground.

When the veterans camped out in 1933 during Franklin Roosevelt's first year in office, Eleanor went as her husband's representative to talk with them. She recalled that they asked her to join them in their dining hall. There she spoke about her experiences helping soldiers during World War I. The veterans responded by singing old army songs to her. Upon leaving, she wished them luck and they wished her the same. One veteran, moved by the First Lady's appearance, said, "Hoover sent the Army. Roosevelt sent his wife."[4]

Her hard work had just begun. In these worst months of the Depression, Eleanor advocated better working conditions for all. She called for an end to child labor and asked women not to patronize sweatshops. She also demonstrated to Americans how they could make inexpensive but nutritious meals. And she urged the United States to take a lead in world affairs.

Continuing her work as the President's eyes and hands, Roosevelt went on numerous trips to observe conditions in which different Americans lived. At one time or another the First Lady talked with farm workers, visited the mentally ill in institutions, and examined the treatment of inmates in American prisons.

In the fall of 1933, at the request of some members of the Society of Friends (also known as Quakers), she toured the coal-mining areas of West Virginia. Eleanor was appalled by what she found. She discovered children who had no idea what it was like to have a decent meal and men who had not worked steadily in five years. She witnessed children sleeping on rags on floors or on beds with no mattresses—blankets were just thrown over bedsprings.

She saw families who did not have shoes, houses caked with coal dust, and children playing in filth-ridden streams. Some men who had previously gone on strike to protest poor working conditions and low wages were being punished by not being hired by any employer. Eleanor found these men and their families living in tents since they could not afford to live in even the shabbiest of houses.

After Eleanor told the President what she had seen, the Roosevelt Administration created self-supporting homestead developments called Arthurdale and Reedsville in the West Virginia mining regions. Eleanor exercised considerable influence over the planning of these model towns. As a result they became the best known of many such projects and model communities established during the New Deal.

Supported by the federal government, Arthurdale was meant to give poverty-stricken miners and their families a place to live where they could support themselves. The fifty families who lived at Arthurdale did so by farming and selling handmade crafts typical of the area. The community operated with a school, town hall, and post office.

There were plans to add a government-owned factory to the community, but conservatives in Congress voted against funding it. They claimed that Arthurdale promoted a form of socialistic government. This opposition, along with serious doubts about Arthurdale's feasibility by some members of Franklin's administration, killed the project. Eleanor blamed the defeat on members of Congress who were ignorant about the miners' situation and even after the homestead was closed down she never lost faith in its idea.[5]

Eleanor's compassion for the underprivileged did not stop with people on the U.S. mainland. In 1934 she journeyed with a group of women reporters to the Caribbean and found the conditions of island residents to be even worse than those she had seen in West Virginia.

In Puerto Rico (a U.S. commonwealth), she witnessed large families crowded into houses with only two rooms. They had no plumbing, no screens on windows or doors to keep out insects, and no indoor kitchens. In many cases goats and other animals lived under houses, which clung to the sides of cliffs.

At Eleanor's urging, Franklin sent government officials and businessmen to Puerto Rico to help the residents develop new industries. She also spoke of a bright future for Puerto Rico as a tourist destination, something nonexistent at the time in what was an under-developed island.

In the second volume of her autobiography *This I Remember* she wrote, " . . . as soon as swimming pools and beaches are available and hotels begin to improve and transportation becomes easier, I think people will find it a very satisfactory and accessible spot."[6] She wrote those words in 1949 and her prediction has come true.

Roosevelt also continued her advocacy of women's issues, pleading with women to become active in politics. In a book called *It's Up to the Women,* she wrote that a woman's "understanding heart" and "vitality" together gave promise of social change.[7]

Eleanor's liberal activism did make her some enemies, not the least of which was cousin Alice. Alice had become well known in political circles for imitating the First Lady's voice and mannerisms in a comical way. Early in the Roosevelt Administration the family had a get-together and Alice was invited.

Instead of showing anger toward her cousin, Eleanor

was gracious and reacted to her cousin's antics with a sense of humor. She asked Alice to do her imitation in front of the group. Then she promptly thanked her cousin for the helpful presentation.

Not all her critics were respectable. There were many narrow-minded people who referred to her as a "nigger-lover" and "Jew-lover" for her work on behalf of oppressed minorities. In the 1930s African-American men and women had few job choices and most were resigned to domestic or manual labor such as cooks, maids, elevator operators, or farm workers. In most of the South racial segregation was the law, and black students could not attend school with whites, including state universities. The idea of an African-American doctor or engineer was unheard of.

In Eleanor Roosevelt's mail, along with countless letters of appreciation, were a sizable number of hate letters condemning her and her social actions. Some were written by people who lacked the courage to sign their names, and Roosevelt ignored those.

A large number of Americans reacted by telling malicious racist jokes about Roosevelt. Rumors spread that she was starting "Eleanor Clubs" in which she was working to replace black female domestic workers with white women.[8]

A firm belief among many Americans, especially in the South, was that blacks belonged in their "proper place," meaning positions subservient to whites. They were distressed by the idea of African Americans not doing domestic work, for which they felt they were best suited.

Interestingly, Eleanor grew up believing some of the same stereotypes about African Americans and Jews. As she matured and became educated, however, she began to think matters over rather than rush to conclusions. In time she saw bigotry as a result of people's envy and insecurity. "When a person holds deep prejudice, he gets to dislike the objects of his prejudice. He uses it as an excuse of something unworthy in himself," she said.[9]

In 1939 Roosevelt put her beliefs into action and made many enemies. A distinguished African-American opera singer named Marian Anderson, known as one of the best in her field, planned a concert in Washington, D.C. A huge crowd was expected to attend.

The only auditorium big enough to accommodate the expected crowd was Constitution Hall, which was under the control of an organization called the Daughters of the American Revolution (DAR). The DAR consisted of descendants of Revolutionary War veterans. Eleanor Roosevelt herself was a member.

Because Anderson was an African American, the DAR refused to permit her to sing in the hall. In protest Roosevelt resigned from the DAR. She wrote at the time, "To remain as a member implies approval of [that] action, and therefore I am resigning."[10]

A poll of the American public taken shortly

afterward showed that 67 percent of Americans agreed with her. In response Roosevelt helped arrange for Anderson to give a free concert at a most appropriate place—the foot of the Lincoln Memorial. Anderson sang a selection of songs, including an African-American spiritual called "Nobody Knows the Trouble I've Seen," as well as "America." Over 75,000 people attended.

Eleanor Roosevelt championed other causes that helped the conditions of African Americans. She urged the appointment of an African-American educator named Mary McLeod Bethune to a government agency called the National Youth Administration.

She also supported an anti-lynching bill. Lynching of blacks in the South was common. But because her husband relied on the votes of all Americans, including southern whites, Franklin would not publicly support his wife's efforts. However, he never publicly objected to her causes.

Until this time most African Americans had traditionally voted Republican. After all the Republican party had been the party of Abraham Lincoln and the abolitionists. However, because of Eleanor Roosevelt's support of black causes and New Deal social programs, African Americans shifted in large numbers to the Democratic party. To this day the majority of African Americans vote Democratic.

There was another change in tradition engineered by the Roosevelts. Franklin Roosevelt ran for an unprecedented third term as President in 1940. Eleanor did not want him to run again. But with war raging in Europe, and Americans concerned about their country's possible role in that war, Franklin felt an obligation to run for the good of the country. So the First Lady supported him.

Eleanor herself had her share of backers and some felt she would make a fine President. A few years earlier, though, she told Louis Howe that the country was not ready for a woman in the Oval Office. Opponents of the Roosevelts believed a third term would afford the President too much power and some distributed political buttons reading, "We don't want Eleanor either."

Again a vocal critic was cousin Alice, who strongly opposed a third term. Eleanor took it all with a grain of salt and wrote in her autobiography, "Neither Franklin nor I ever minded the disagreeable things my cousin Alice Longworth used to say during the various campaigns, though some of the people around Franklin resented them bitterly."[11] In spite of the critics Franklin went on to win the election in another landslide.

For a while it looked as though Alice and Eleanor would engage in a war of printed as well as spoken words. In 1936 both were writing columns distributed by rival newspaper syndicates (groups of newspapers). Eleanor's column commonly focused on her concern for others while Alice's was filled with sarcasm and biting criticisms of both Eleanor and other political opponents.

Fellow journalists found the rivalry amusing. At a meeting of the Women's National Press Club in 1936, a skit called "Alice or Eleanor, or These Little Girls Make Big Money" was presented. Actresses portrayed the two women sitting at their desks. On Roosevelt's desk was a bottle of maple syrup while on Longworth's was a bottle of vinegar.

The rivalry was short-lived, however, since Longworth decided journalism was not for her and quit writing soon afterward. Roosevelt loved her work as a journalist and continued it for the rest of her life. While she had written some magazine articles in the 1920s it was as First Lady in 1934 that Roosevelt began writing a regular column called "Mrs. Roosevelt's Page." It appeared monthly in a magazine called *Woman's Home Companion*.

A little over a year later she began writing a daily column called "My Day." It ran in newspapers across the country, and she would write it for the rest of her life. Her first writings dwelled on aspects of her social life such as parties and family.

In time Roosevelt started to discuss her opinions on important issues of the day. Franklin often used the column as a "trial balloon" to test his ideas. He would make official decisions based on the public's reaction to his wife's words. Before long, political opponents would read "My Day" to pick up hints on the President's plans.

In her "My Day" column for Monday, December 8,

1941, Roosevelt wrote, "I was going out in the hall to say goodbye to our cousins . . . and, as I stepped out of my room, I knew something had happened."[12]

Roosevelt was referring to the attack by Japan on the U.S. Naval Base at Pearl Harbor, Hawaii. On December 8 the President declared war on Japan in words that are famous: "Yesterday, December 7, 1941—a date which will live in infamy—the United States of America was suddenly and deliberately attacked by naval and air forces of the Empire of Japan."[13]

Three days later Germany, allied with Japan, declared war on the United States, and the United States was now an active participant in World War II.

A few months earlier, in the fall of 1941, Eleanor Roosevelt was given her first official government position, co-director for the Office of Civilian Defense. At the time the United States had not yet entered the war. However, Europe and the Far East were in turmoil, and Americans felt preparedness in case of war was necessary.

Roosevelt's opinion was that mobilization for war went beyond military preparedness to include social needs. This included proper nutrition, decent housing, and satisfactory health care for all citizens. Her opponents felt that she was incorporating her husband's New Deal policies into her position and claimed that her welfare programs would lead to socialism in the United States. A lesser known person in her position would likely have gotten a fraction of the publicity and complaints that the First Lady received. Eleanor felt the criticism was starting to cloud the intentions of her husband's administration and she resigned under pressure in February 1942.

Eleanor admitted that the administration's New Deal programs were important to her because of all the good she believed they were doing for the poor and unemployed. In fact, when the president, referring to himself, later announced that "Dr. Win-the-War" had replaced "Dr. New Deal," she expressed her regret. Eleanor had hoped that the New Deal policies would continue and be given emphasis into the war years.[14]

As she did during World War I, Eleanor helped during the war effort in ways with which she was familiar. As she had done for West Virginia miners several years earlier, Roosevelt paid visits to those who needed help. This time it was people touched by the war.

First and foremost there were the fighting men. She made three journeys abroad to inspect the troops and visit the wounded in hospitals. In 1942 she flew to bomb-scarred London. There she alternated official meetings with Prime Minister Winston Churchill and King George VI with taking walks in rain and mud with soldiers. She also made time to visit Red Cross clubs and took a special interest in learning how women in the British military were being trained.

Over the next few years Eleanor made trips to see

American troops in the South Pacific and the Caribbean. At first, top military personnel were reluctant to let her into the more dangerous locations. One was the island of Guadalcanal, where a bloody six-month-long battle had ended just months earlier. But the officials relented, and Eleanor shook hands with injured men, signed autographs, and even took messages from the wounded to their loved ones.

Admiral William Halsey later wrote, "I marveled at her hardihood, both physical and mental. She walked for miles, and she saw patients who were grievously and gruesomely wounded. . . . She alone had accomplished more good than any other person, or any group of civilians, who had passed through my area."[15]

Roosevelt's trips were not limited to those in combat. She comforted residents on the U.S. west coast, who felt Los Angeles or San Francisco might be the next Pearl Harbor. And she offered her sympathy to Japanese Americans living in internment camps in the remote Arizona desert.

In an act of wartime hysteria, the U.S. government had forced over 110,000 Japanese Americans to be taken from their homes and moved to war relocation camps. Some people believed that people of Japanese descent living in the United States were a threat to the country. But there was no truth to this belief, and in 1976 President Gerald Ford issued an official proclamation condemning the unfair wartime act. In 1988 Congress

During World War II, Eleanor Roosevelt made several trips to see American troops. Here, Roosevelt (second from right) is greeted by American officials on a trip to the South Pacific.

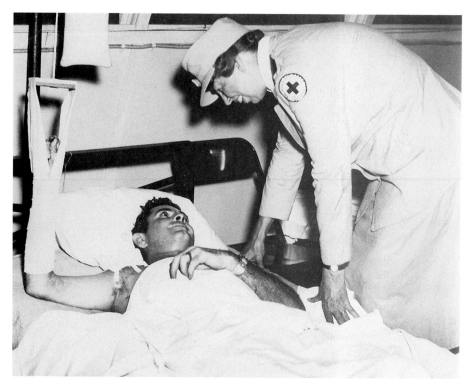

Roosevelt took time during the war to visit with injured soldiers, shake their hands, sign autographs, and even take messages from them to their loved ones.

authorized monetary compensation to persons of Japanese ancestry who were evacuated, relocated, or interned during World War II.

Furthermore, Roosevelt also lobbied strongly for better treatment of African Americans in the armed forces and more liberal immigration policies for war refugees from other countries.

Eleanor Roosevelt was not a resident of the White House when Japan surrendered in August 1945, ending the war. On April 12, 1945, just five months after winning a fourth term as President, Franklin Roosevelt died suddenly of a cerebral hemorrhage at his retreat in Warm Springs, Georgia. Warm Springs was the location of a spa where he often went for polio treatments. Eleanor was attending a benefit when she received a telephone call from an adviser with the news.

After telling Roosevelt of her husband's death, the presidential press secretary announced to reporters Roosevelt first words: "I am more sorry for the people of this country and of the world than I am for ourselves."[16]

She then sent a telegram to her sons that read, "Darlings: Father slept away this afternoon. He did his job to the end as he would want you to do."[17]

Soon afterward she uncovered a distressing fact. Lucy Mercer Rutherfurd, who had married but was now a widow and single, was with Franklin when he died. Eleanor also learned that her daughter Anna knew that

The spa where Franklin Roosevelt often went in Warm Springs, Georgia. In 1945, he died here suddenly of a cerebral hemorrhage.

Lucy had visited Franklin in the White House. But Anna insisted that the relationship had long settled into one of friendship and not romance. Of course, Eleanor was outraged; but in time, the bitterness eased. A letter written by Eleanor to Anna just over a month after Franklin's death showed no hard feelings.[18]

Diplomat

A few days after the death of her husband, Roosevelt said to a reporter, "The story is over."[1] She was wrong; the story was far from over. Roosevelt was to continue her husband's legacy and her own career.

For most other First Ladies the story would have been over. Upon the deaths of their husbands, the majority settled into private life and rarely appeared in public. But Eleanor Roosevelt was not a typical First Lady.

Roosevelt originally planned on devoting her time to her journalism career. Soon the new President, Harry Truman, had another idea. Just months after her husband's death, Roosevelt was called by Truman and asked to serve as a delegate to the first meeting of the General Assembly of the UN.

The UN was an organization that had been chartered in 1945 at an international conference in San Francisco, California. Truman knew how much both Franklin and Eleanor cherished the idea of this body of nations solving their problems through an open forum.

Roosevelt declined at first, saying she had no experience in foreign affairs. After Truman's insistence, though, she finally relented. The President saw her selection to this post as a tribute to her husband. But he also recognized her natural understanding of others and her basic good will. He knew those would be perfect qualifications for the job.

By the end of the year Roosevelt was on her way to London, where the first UN meetings were to take place in January 1946. In her column "My Day" dated January 5, 1946, and written enroute to London, she wrote:

> I have been thinking of the grave responsibility which lies not only on the delegates to the United Nations Organization but on the nation as a whole as we gather for our first meeting of the UNO Assembly. On the success or failure of the United Nations Organization may depend the preservation and continuance of our civilization.[2]

No one at the time, other than perhaps personal friends, could have known that deep down Roosevelt was frightened about her new job. Years later she candidly confessed, "I was feeling rather lost and quite

The United Nations headquarters in New York City. While the early meetings of the UN were held in Europe, the site was eventually moved to this location in New York.

uncertain about what lay ahead." And she referred to herself as "a confused beginner in such affairs."[3]

She also recalled the drudgery of poring over official documents, sounding much like a student forced by a teacher to read a boring textbook. "I promptly sat down and began reading—or trying to read. It was dull reading and very hard work. I had great difficulty in staying awake, but I knew my duty when I saw it and read them all."[4]

Roosevelt was aware that by being the only woman on the United States delegation she faced increased pressure. Many men in 1946 disapproved of the idea of a woman sitting on such an important committee. Roosevelt knew that if she failed it might appear that women were not capable of this kind of diplomatic work.

To help prove the worthiness of women, Roosevelt invited the women from all the other delegations to tea. With them she discussed several topics, ranging from social chitchat to difficult parts of their jobs. She found much could be accomplished in small meetings on the semi-social level. Roosevelt continued these get-togethers during the seven years she was associated with the UN.

There were times when she had to speak in formal sessions. And on one occasion she came head to head with one of the most powerful men of the Soviet Union delegation. Roosevelt had been assigned by the U.S. delegation to serve on the Economic and Social

Committee (known officially as Committee 3) of the General Assembly. The delegation thought that Committee 3 was one of the least important ones. And they believed a woman of little experience had less chance to encounter any vital political issues there.

But a committee problem concerning war refugees snowballed into a major flare-up. Roosevelt was placed in a starring role on the center stage of diplomatic relations opposite Andrei Vishinsky. She referred to Vishinsky as "one of the Russians' great legal minds, a skilled debater, a man with ability to use the weapons of wit and ridicule."[5]

At the end of World War II there were many displaced war refugees originally from parts of the Soviet Union, Poland, Czechoslovakia, and other countries. In addition there were numerous Jewish survivors of Nazi death camps living in makeshift shelters in Germany. Not wanting to live under communism, the refugees decided it was better to stay in their temporary housing than return to their native countries.

The Soviets and their communist bloc allies demanded that all war refugees be returned to the countries they came from. They claimed those who did not return to their native countries were traitors. The United States and their western European allies argued that these refugees were no different than any other human beings who had the right to choose where they wanted to live.

The Soviets thought that this was such an important issue that they did not let the Soviet representative on Committee 3 state their position to the General Assembly. Instead, they gave the assignment to the head of the entire Soviet Union delegation, the brilliant Andrei Vishinsky.

He spoke before the assembly on two different occasions, defending the Soviet point of view. The Americans needed a speaker to counter Vishinsky. Since Roosevelt was more familiar with the refugee problem than any other U.S. delegate, she was selected to represent her country.

Roosevelt never let her true emotions show since a strong performance was vital. But she later wrote, "I was badly frightened. I trembled at the thought of speaking against the famous Mr. Vishinsky. But when the time came I walked, tense and excited, to the rostrum and did my best."[6]

Knowing that her side needed the votes of the South American countries, Roosevelt purposely mentioned a famous soldier and political liberator of South America named Simón Bolívar. She emphasized his stands for the freedom of his people.

It was later in the day when Roosevelt spoke. She knew that the Soviets were hoping some delegates who supported the view of the United States, such as the South Americans, would leave out of weariness. But Roosevelt's references to Bolívar electrified the South

American delegates. They stayed until the end of her speech and voted with the United States and its western allies. The resolution permitting the refugees to choose the country in which they wished to live passed.

The refugee situation would not be solved overnight, but Roosevelt wrote, "the principle of the right of an individual to make his own decisions was a victory well worth while."[7] As events turned out Vishinsky raised the same issue in subsequent meetings. But he could never muster enough votes to counter the original decision brought about by Roosevelt.

Arthur H. Vandenberg and John Foster Dulles were two Republican members of the American delegation who had opposed Roosevelt's presence at the UN. They perceived the world of diplomacy as "man's business." Near the end of the sessions in London they went to speak with Roosevelt.

When writing later about this incident, Roosevelt could not recall which man did the speaking. But she felt that whichever one did, spoke for both men. He said:

> Mrs. Roosevelt, we must tell you that we did all we could to keep you off the United States delegation. We begged the President not to nominate you. But now that you are leaving we feel we must acknowledge that we have worked with you gladly and found you good to work with. And we will be happy to do so again.[8]

Before returning to her home in New York,

Roosevelt flew to Germany at the request of the U.S Army. The Army had called upon her to pay tribute to the six million Jews murdered during the Holocaust. While in Germany she was asked by a German reporter whether she thought all Germans should be blamed for the war and its deadly results.

Roosevelt later wrote, "I answered what to me seems obvious. All the people of Germany have to accept responsibility for having trusted a leadership which first brought such misery to groups of people within their own nation and later created world chaos."[9]

Back in the United States, Roosevelt did not slow down. She continued her journalism career, writing "My Day" as well as a monthly column for the magazine *Ladies' Home Journal.* She also completed the second volume of her memoirs, *This I Remember.* Appearances on radio and television were frequent, too, making for an exhaustive schedule.

The hectic lifestyle caught up with her in August 1946, when the car she was driving collided with another car while enroute from her home at Val-Kill to New York City. She immediately took full blame for the accident; she had become drowsy while driving. Luckily her injuries were minor. She suffered mostly bruises and two broken front teeth.

Even after the accident, while still in pain and shock, Roosevelt wrote her column, handling the scary event with a sense of humor. "Now I shall have two lovely porcelain [front teeth], which will look far better than the rather protruding large teeth which most of the Roosevelts have."[10]

Within a few months Roosevelt resumed her duties with the UN. Shortly afterward President Truman named her chair of the UN Commission on Human Rights. The long tedious task of drafting the "Universal Declaration of Human Rights" had begun. Over two years later, and after eighty-five meetings of Committee 3 in 1948 alone, the declaration was at long last adopted.[11]

With human rights and the welfare of others always on her mind, Roosevelt became known for her criticism of communism and her support for the new nation of Israel. Throughout her public career, some of her fiercest critics accused her of having communist leanings or ties. But they were wrong. She wrote and publicly announced her strong disdain for the then Soviet Union and the communist system.

Roosevelt put her words into actions. She played an important role in the founding of a liberal political action committee called Americans for Democratic Action (ADA), which prohibited communists from leadership positions. In doing so, she broke ranks with the ultra-liberal Henry Wallace, her husband's former Vice President and Truman's secretary of commerce. Wallace's own group, the Progressive Citizens of America (PCA) was criticized by Roosevelt for not

Eleanor Roosevelt holds a poster of the Declaration of Human Rights. It was through her dedication and hard work that the declaration was adopted.

enacting such a rule. Roosevelt had hoped liberal groups could work together, but she would not work with the PCA as long as it kept communists in major roles. Her criticism of Wallace's group helped cement her and the ADA as the real heirs to her husband's legacy.

Still she was conciliatory. Believing that as long as the United States had to live with the Soviets, she thought they may as well try to live peacefully alongside them.

Now and then her beliefs in her principles led to disagreements with friends—even President Truman. The subject of one such dispute was the Middle East.

When World War II ended, the land called Palestine (today mostly comprising the countries of Israel and Jordan) was a mandate, or territory, under British rule. At that time Jews had no homeland, although many were living in Palestine as well as in numerous other countries in which they were minorities. Also residing in Palestine were Arabs who had been at home there for generations.

Many Jews wished to live in a country where they could govern themselves. Those Jews felt Palestine should be their homeland for a variety of reasons. Some believed that Palestine was the Biblical homeland of the Jews and therefore it should also be their modern home. But more cited the Balfour Declaration, a 1917 document from the British government supporting a Jewish homeland in Palestine. Many Palestinian Arabs opposed a Jewish state there, saying it would infringe upon their rights.

At first Roosevelt opposed a Jewish state in Palestine. She believed, as her husband did, that the territory was not big enough to absorb a substantial number of immigrants. But Jewish refugees, including many survivors of Nazi death camps, set out toward Palestine. There they were barred entry by the British and sent to refugee camps elsewhere.

Most of the world's citizens supported the Jewish refugees, and in time, Roosevelt also did. In 1946 the General Assembly of the UN took a vote on the Jewish refugee matter. When they voted to study the situation further rather than settling it right away, Roosevelt was disappointed. She made her feelings public in "My Day," stating that further study was unnecessary and would only cause prolonged suffering for the refugees.

The General Assembly study recommended that Palestine be divided into two states, one Jewish and one Arab. The city of Jerusalem, which is holy to both Jews and Muslims, would be administered separately by the UN. The majority of General Assembly member nations, including the United States, voted in favor of the two-nation plan. But the Arab nations wouldn't accept any agreement that included a Jewish state and planned to occupy Palestine by force.

Oil companies and other special interests pressured the United States to change its policy of support for the plan. Roosevelt voiced her anger at this to the President. She argued that opposing the UN vote would weaken the UN. If the United States disregarded a UN vote, then what would stop other countries from doing the same? If this precedent was set, then soon the UN would be worthless.

She added that parting from an official vote would hurt not only the UN and the Jewish people, but also the Democratic party. If the UN collapsed, she reasoned, voters would associate it with the failed League of Nations and tag Truman as a failure as well.

To keep the peace, Roosevelt felt a UN police force made up of members of the armed forces of different countries should be sent to Palestine. The U.S. Defense Department opposed this idea since it meant American soldiers would have to serve alongside those from the Soviet Union.

Roosevelt called this objection "complete nonsense," and told President Truman she was ready to resign her position as U.S. delegate to the UN.[12]

Truman begged her to stay. He said that her resignation would be disastrous for the new body struggling for acceptance. Roosevelt then traveled to London for a month on personal business. Upon her return she again offered her resignation if the United States withdrew its support of the two-country plan. President Truman was very concerned.

As events turned out Truman did not need to make

any decision regarding her threat. A combination of Soviet support and British acceptance of the two-nation plan led the American special interest groups to drop their opposition. They felt that even if the United States changed its vote, they would be outnumbered by the other member nations.

On May 11, 1948, Roosevelt learned that the Soviet Union was about to recognize the state of Israel. The United States never wanted to be second to the Soviets in anything. Thanks to Roosevelt's information (as well as domestic considerations with an upcoming presidential election near), Truman immediately publicly recognized the Jewish state, edging out the Soviets in being the first to do so.

This woman who wielded influence and courted respect from world leaders, including the President of the United States, hardly seemed like the timid and self-conscious little girl who was too scared to spell words aloud in school.

8

First Lady of the World

Roosevelt loved her work for the UN and continued it in some capacity until 1952.[1] President Truman decided not to run for another term in the White House that year. The Democratic candidate, governor of Illinois Adlai Stevenson, lost the presidential election to Republican candidate Dwight D. Eisenhower. A five-star general and hero of World War II, Eisenhower was incredibly popular, and Roosevelt was not surprised at his easy victory.[2]

She was initially warm to the idea of an Eisenhower presidency, in spite of the fact that he was a Republican. But during the course of the presidential campaign, Roosevelt became disenchanted with the former general. She felt that the views he expressed were more in keeping with those of extreme conservatives.[3] Near the end of the campaign she gave a speech harshly criticizing Eisenhower.

After Eisenhower was elected she felt that it would be best to step down. This way the new President could appoint someone of his own party to her post.

Typically her farewell speech to the UN was about women's rights, although her message went beyond simply asking for equality. She urged that more women be allowed in decision-making processes and lamented the fact that most important government policies in all countries were made by men.

After resigning she did not completely cut ties with the UN. Shortly after offering her resignation Roosevelt volunteered to work with the American Association for the United Nations. This organization was not affiliated with the government, but lobbied to gain support for the UN and its ideals.

In fact, Roosevelt never held a government post again, although she did have many occasions to make her opinions known. She was much in demand as a speaker and advocate. Of course, she continued writing both "My Day" and her monthly magazine column.

The early 1950s were hard years for liberals such as Roosevelt. In the United States there was intense fear of communism being spread abroad. Some powerful Americans were, as a saying pointed out, looking for communist spies under every rock at home. Many of these people accused any American who had ever attended a labor union meeting or a left-wing gathering of being a communist capable of treason. Thus the majority of the accused were in no way affiliated with the communist party.

The most famous of the anti-communist crusaders was Republican Senator Joseph McCarthy of Wisconsin. The communist scare began in the late 1940s. But it was in 1953 when, as head of the Senate Subcommittee on Investigations, McCarthy led hearings in which he questioned Americans accused of being communists. In most cases there was little or no evidence to prove the charges. With the fear of communism as strong as it was, many of these people were simply assumed guilty by accusation.

A large number had their reputations ruined. Many also lost their jobs, and therefore, were unable to earn a living. Employers simply did not want to take a chance on hiring a suspected communist.

For example, in 1952 eight public school teachers suspected of being communists were fired from their jobs. A Supreme Court decision in March of that year legalized such firings. In addition, many Hollywood actors and screenwriters suspected of supporting communism were blacklisted. Being blacklisted meant that they were not hired for work because of their supposed communist links.

McCarthy went on to make the outrageous claim that U.S. government agencies were filled with communist spies. In this time of fear and panic he was widely believed. (The practice of accusing persons of disloyalty or any other illegal or immoral act without hard evidence to back up such claims has since become known as McCarthyism.)

People avoided attending meetings of left-wing groups or labor unions for fear of being accused of having communist ties. Roosevelt was appalled by the spread of these fears as well as by Senator McCarthy's techniques. As early as April 1950, Roosevelt said in a speech to the Americans for Democratic Action, "The day I'm afraid to sit down with people I do not know because five years from now someone will say five of those people were Communists and therefore you are a Communist—that will be a bad day."[4]

Some of Roosevelt's political enemies wanted her to appear before McCarthy's committee, but the senator never called her. Perhaps he realized even he couldn't succeed in bullying this accomplished diplomat and former First Lady. In her bold manner she defended McCarthy's targets whom she knew were innocent, including civil rights leaders who felt they were next in line to be accused. She flatly stated that some people on the far right were exploiting McCarthy's fear tactics. She said that they would gladly "label anything they don't like as communist."[5]

While Roosevelt vocally opposed McCarthy she was careful to let Americans know she was still as opposed to communism as she always had been. In "My Day" published February 16, 1951, she wrote:

> I would not look for a communist under every bed. I would believe that the vast majority of our people believe in their republican form of government and their democratic way of life. I will accept the fact that we have to improve and constantly try to give benefits to more people within our own nation, but I will not believe that the terror and poverty of communism and their faith in materialism instead of in God can win in the struggle in which we are now engaged.[6]

The public and the politicians finally had enough of McCarthy following his televised inquisition of the Army. His influence ended in 1954 when he was censured by the U.S. Senate.

For a while it seemed as though Roosevelt was constantly courting controversy. In 1949 she was involved in a well-publicized dispute with Francis Joseph Cardinal Spellman, the leading Catholic clergyman in the United States. He had accused her of being anti-Catholic.

What triggered Spellman's allegeation was Roosevelt's opposition to federal aid to parochial schools. Roosevelt was a firm believer in the separation of church and state. She believed that any parent had the right to send his or her children to a school run by a church or synagogue. On the other hand, she felt that it was unfair to expect the money from taxpayers of varied religions to pay for someone else's religious education.

But she had other opinions that also angered Spellman. Roosevelt favored birth control, which was against official Catholic policy. When a magazine called *Nation* published articles attacking the political views of the Catholic church leadership, church leaders in New York City asked public schools to ban the magazine from their libraries. A true believer in civil liberties and freedom of speech, Roosevelt aggressively protested the proposed ban.

In a letter to Roosevelt, Spellman wrote " . . . your record of anti-Catholicism stands for all to see," and he accused her of being "unworthy of an American mother."[7]

Roosevelt wrote back a personal letter, claiming to harbor no bigotry toward any religion and concluding with, "I assure you that I had no sense of being 'an unworthy American mother.' The final judgment, my dear Cardinal Spellman, of the unworthiness of all human beings is in the hands of God."[8]

Roosevelt received thousands of letters at her Val-Kill home—most of them favorable—including many from Catholics who wrote in her defense. The disagreement approached an end when a representative of the church paid a personal visit to Val-Kill and clarified Spellman's positions. He said the cardinal did not expect the general public to support religious schools. He only wanted help to defray the costs of "auxiliary services" such as textbooks. Shortly afterward Cardinal Spellman stopped by Roosevelt's home for a talk. The two parted amiably.

The controversies followed Roosevelt in those fearful times. She tried breaking into broadcasting in the early 1950s, hosting at different times radio and television discussion programs. But she was unable to get sponsors. Companies feared potential trouble stirred up by the extreme right wing.

By today's standards, there was not anything even slightly controversial about Roosevelt's programs. In fact, some of the strongest objections were heard when she tried to schedule Paul Robeson, a well-respected African-American performer as a guest on her television show. Blacks at that time were simply not seen on television in roles equal to whites. In addition it was known that Robeson supported left-wing organizations. Her plan to have a left-wing African-American guest was so explosive that at the network's request she had Robeson's appearance canceled.

Still, polls showed that average Americans had a great deal of respect for the former First Lady and diplomat. Though conservative activists and anti-communist zealots feared Roosevelt, the general public greatly admired her. In 1948 the magazine *Women's Home Companion* asked readers, "What American—man or woman—now living do you admire most?" Eleanor Roosevelt emerged first, beating out popular generals such as Eisenhower, George Marshall, and Douglas MacArthur as well as President Harry Truman.[9]

In a poll taken in the fall of 1951 she was voted "the greatest living American woman."[10] Roosevelt would continue to lead such American polls until and even after her death. In a poll conducted of 1,000 women by the magazine *Ladies' Home Journal* in September 1988, Eleanor Roosevelt was selected as the most admired First Lady in U.S. history. This was nearly twenty-six years after she died and forty-three years after she left the White House.[11]

Her popularity overseas was as great as it was at home. Roosevelt spent many of her later years traveling to faraway places such as Israel, Pakistan, India, Scandinavia, and the former countries of Yugoslavia and the Soviet Union. She often took her grandchildren with her, and they received a real education. These trips were far different than those of a typical tourist.

One granddaughter, Nina Roosevelt Gibson, recalled trips taken with her grandmother when she was in her teens. Gibson remembered:

> When we were in established cities [like Paris or Rome or London] she usually had . . . business-type things, either for the UN or for some specific reason that we were there. But for my purposes she would show me the city, not so much

In a 1951 poll, Eleanor Roosevelt was voted "the greatest living American woman." Here, she is shown (first row, second from left) surrounded by notables at an award luncheon. (Her friend, vocalist Marian Anderson is seated in the first row, second from right.)

the way the ordinary tourists would see it, but sometimes through the hospitals, through meeting all sorts of people, and then the museums, too. . . .

In Israel she wanted me to see the Red Sea and a lot of the biblical attractions and made sure that tours were set up so that I could do that. But she also wanted me to be a part of her trips to various schools, to hospitals, to factories and just out in the countryside, too. I think she wanted to make sure that I had an appreciation for the Arabs who lived in Israel at the time . . . so we saw how the Arabs lived, which of course was fascinating to me.[12]

Having a famous and well-loved grandmother had other benefits, such as a personal and informal visit with Queen Elizabeth II of England in London. "We got in a taxi," Gibson recalled, "and Grandmere [Roosevelt] said, 'Buckingham Palace, please.' And that undid me. I mean that only happens in storybooks! We got there, and it was just the queen, my grandmother, and me."[13]

Another grandchild, John Boettiger, remembered a trip to Europe with his grandmother when he was a teenager and she was in her early seventies:

We were moving through the countryside with her and everywhere she went she was sought out by the local figures and celebrated, and [she] felt the responsibility of appropriate response. It was more difficult for us as kids to feel that obligation.

Particularly at the end of a long day of travel, we really wanted to collapse into whatever entertainment there might be around or maybe just into bed. [Her] energy was still considerable at the end of the day, more considerable than a couple of teenage grandchildren.[14]

When not overseas or involved in some official business function, Roosevelt could be found in either of her two residences, in New York City or at Val-Kill. But although she had two addresses, it was at Val-Kill where she could truly relax and be herself.

The atmosphere was informal and friendly there. Roosevelt was often found sitting on a wicker chair on the porch while family and friends cooked hot dogs using an outdoor fireplace. The spirit was so easy-going that a respected world leader such as British Prime Minister Winston Churchill thought nothing of dropping formalities to take a soothing swim in the outdoor pool before grabbing a hot dog for lunch. There were other renowned guests who came to Val-Kill too, including then Massachusetts Senator John F. Kennedy, Soviet Premier Nikita Khrushchev, and Yugoslavia's leader Marshal Tito.

The piano she kept in the living room is symbolic of Roosevelt's care and concern for others. She could not play, but her children and grandchildren could. So she kept it for their use. And like most grandmothers, she went out of her way to accommodate her grandchildren. She offered them freshly baked cookies. Or she might read aloud Rudyard Kipling tales while the young ones relaxed on the flower-print chairs in the living room.

John Boettiger remembers that his grandmother's hospitality extended to children not her own. In a manner similar to the way she helped her father aid the poor when she was a little girl, Roosevelt hosted picnics at Val-Kill for students from the Wiltwyck School for Boys, a special school for underprivileged children.

Boettiger looked back into his memories and said:

> My vision of her is almost a series of snapshots, reading or entertaining or talking with the Wiltwyck kids out on the lawn—serving hamburgers and hot dogs—or her in that wonderful, kind of long, old-fashioned bathing suit, coming up to the edge of the pool and doing a big, slow belly flopper and then swimming very deliberately from one end to the other.[15]

Boettiger added a comment reflecting on one of his grandmother's earliest fears, that of water, and how she never gave up trying to come to terms with it. "I don't think she ever finally triumphed over her adversary relationship to the water, but she was determined to master it."[16]

Although she did not actively campaign for the Democrats in the 1952 presidential election, she made one last full-steam burst into political life in 1956. Adlai Stevenson was again nominated as the Democratic candidate to run against President Eisenhower.

Roosevelt explained that she re-entered the political scene in 1956 because of her intense respect for

Eleanor Roosevelt with presidential candidate Adlai Stevenson in 1956. Roosevelt worked doggedly for the unsuccessful campaign.

Stevenson and her disappointment in what she saw as the lack of progress during Eisenhower's four years.[17]

She worked doggedly for the Stevenson campaign. She rushed from one town to another, made speeches, and spoke with the press. At the Democratic Convention in Chicago, Roosevelt implored her party to march beyond the New Deal to the point of wiping out poverty in America. Edward R. Murrow, one of the most renowned news correspondents of all time, called her address "the greatest convention speech I ever heard."[18]

In spite of her efforts, Eisenhower beat Stevenson in another landslide. It was truly a reflection of Eisenhower's popularity, since the Democrats won control of both the House of Representatives and the Senate. Roosevelt later said, "When it was all over, I was glad to be out of politics. I couldn't forget that sometimes my feet hurt during the campaign and that I seldom got enough sleep."[19]

Roosevelt was not as enthusiastic about the 1960 Democratic presidential candidate John F. Kennedy. In part this was because he had not voiced disapproval of Senator Joseph McCarthy. She was hoping Stevenson would run again. Her three Democratic sons supported Kennedy, however. (The fourth surviving son, John, became a Republican.) But when Kennedy got the nomination, she supported him as well.

Eleanor Roosevelt never slowed down; to the end she was active. At the age of seventy-five she became a

Even in retirement, Eleanor Roosevelt kept active politically. Here, Roosevelt (center) accompanies Soviet leader Nikita Khrushchev and his wife on a visit to Franklin Roosevelt's grave in 1959.

visiting professor at Brandeis University outside of Boston. But Roosevelt refused to have her students call her "professor" since she didn't think she deserved that honorable title.[20]

She finally was given a regular television discussion show called *Prospects of Mankind.* And she still wrote "My Day," by then printed in *McCall's* magazine, and several other articles on special assignment.

After a failed U.S.-led invasion of Cuba by Cuban expatriates in 1961—today referred to as the Bay of Pigs Invasion—she served on the Tractors for Freedom Committee. The committee negotiated an exchange of prisoners with Cuban leader Fidel Casto.

She continued to be lured by offers from the White House. President Kennedy asked Roosevelt to take a post on the National Advisory Council of the Peace Corps, a government organization started by Kennedy to aid and train people of developing countries.

And when she felt that President Kennedy was not hiring enough women for government positions, she proudly sent him a three-page list of names of women she considered capable of holding federal posts. In late 1961 she accepted an appointment by Kennedy to preside over the Presidential Commission on the Status of Women.

Eleanor Roosevelt died November 7, 1962, after a short illness, and was buried beside her husband in the rose garden of his Hyde Park mansion. President

Kennedy, Vice-President Lyndon Johnson, and former Presidents Harry Truman and Dwight Eisenhower attended the funeral along with diplomats from the UN.

Roosevelt was eulogized in the most glowing terms by leaders from across the world. United Nations Secretary General U Thant said, "We and the UN salute her memory for her warm humanitarianism and her deep concern for the underprivileged."[21]

Queen Elizabeth II sent her condolences, adding, "The British people held her in deep respect and affection and mourn her passing. My husband and I and my family greatly valued her friendship."[22]

American UN official and 1950 Nobel Peace Prize winner Ralph Bunche called Roosevelt "a beacon of hope and promise for all those throughout the world who are underprivileged and discriminated against, opposed and victimized by forces of prejudice and greed."[23]

As for cousin Alice, she later praised Eleanor, saying that many of her harsh comments were meant to be taken as good-natured kidding. "Eleanor and Franklin shouldn't have minded my making merry of them. I've always laughed about all the family, including myself. I'm a comic character, too."[24]

Specifically she later said that Eleanor "had an extraordinary career. Of all the Presidents' wives, none used her position in quite the same effective way that Eleanor did."[25]

Alice added that without Eleanor, Franklin would have amounted to nothing. One of Alice's friends said though Alice joked about Eleanor, "one got the distinct impression that she [Alice] was proud that Mrs. Roosevelt was a member of the family."[26]

But President Truman might have said it best when he called Eleanor Roosevelt the "First Lady of the World."[27]

Chronology

1884—Born in New York City on October 14.

1892—Mother dies on December 7.

1894—Father dies on August 14.

1899—Attends Allenswood School in London.
-1902

1905—Marries Franklin Delano Roosevelt on March 17.

1906—Daughter Anna is born.

1907—Son James is born.

1909—Son Franklin is born and dies.

1910—Son Elliott is born.

1910—Lives in Albany; first involvement in political
-1912 life.

1912—Moves to Washington, D.C., as husband works for Woodrow Wilson Administration.

1914—Another son named Franklin is born.

1916—Son John is born.

1917—Performs volunteer work during World War I.
-1918

1920—Campaigns for husband as he runs for Vice President.

1921—Franklin contracts polio.

1923—Works with Bok Committee.

1926—Starts Val-Kill Industries.

1927—Begins teaching at Todhunter School.

1929—Moves to Albany as Franklin is elected governor of New York.

1933—After Franklin is elected President of the United States, Eleanor moves to Washington, D.C., as First Lady.

1934—Founds Arthurdale.

1936—Starts writing newspaper column "My Day."

1939—Resigns DAR membership over Marian Anderson controversy; arranges for Anderson to sing at Lincoln Memorial.

1941—Co-director of Office of Civilian Defense.
-1942

1942—On behalf of President, tours American bases
-1944   and visits fighting men during World War II.

1945—Leaves Washington, D.C., after husband dies; lives in New York City and at Val-Kill.

1946—Appointed delegate to UN General Assembly.

1946—Chairs UN Commission on Human Rights.
-1948

1948—"Universal Declaration of Human Rights" adopted.

1949—Conflict with Cardinal Spellman.

1952—Resigns UN position.

1956—Campaigns for Adlai Stevenson for President.

1959—Named visiting professor at Brandeis University.

1961—Serves on Tractors for Freedom Committee after Bay of Pigs incident.

1962—Dies on November 7.

Places to Visit

Hyde Park, New York

Eleanor Roosevelt National Historic Site.
The site consists of Val-Kill and its grounds. Open May through October, daily; March, April, November, and December, weekends only. (914) 229-9115.

Home of Franklin D. Roosevelt National Historic Site.
This is the mansion where Franklin Roosevelt was born and lived much of his adult life. Also here are the Roosevelts' gravesites. Open year-round. (914) 229-9115.

Franklin D. Roosevelt Library and Museum.
The official Roosevelt presidential museum; it includes a wing devoted to Eleanor Roosevelt's life and career. Open year-round. (914) 229-8114.

New York City, New York

United Nations Headquarters.
Guided tours of the complex are offered. Tickets for open meetings of the General Assembly, which begin in late September, are also available. Call for details. Open year-round. (212) 963-1234.

Oyster Bay, New York

Sagamore Hill National Historic Site.
This is the home of Theodore Roosevelt, Eleanor's uncle and 26th President of the United States. As a young girl Eleanor went on family outings here. Open year-round. (516) 922-4447.

Campobello Island, New Brunswick, Canada

Roosevelt Campobello International Park.
The park covers 2,600 acres, but the highlight is the Roosevelt summer home. It was here that Franklin Roosevelt was stricken with polio. The island is connected to the state of Maine by the Franklin D. Roosevelt Memorial Bridge. Open late May through early October. (506) 752-2922.

Warm Springs, Georgia

Little White House State Historic Site.
The retreat where Franklin Roosevelt went for polio therapy treatments; it is the site of his death. Open year-round. (706) 655-3511.

Chapter Notes

Chapter 1

1. A. David Gurewitsch, *Eleanor Roosevelt Her Day*, essay by Dr. William Korey, "Eleanor Roosevelt and the Universal Declaration of Human Rights" (New York: Interchange Foundation, 1973), p. 11.

2. Joseph P. Lash, *"Life Was Meant to Be Lived,"*: *A Centenary Portrait of Eleanor Roosevelt* (New York: W.W. Norton and Co., 1984), pp. 152–153; Gurewitsch, p. 158.

3. Eleanor Roosevelt, *My Day, Volume II: The Post-War Years* (New York: Pharos Books, 1990), p. 119.

4. Eleanor Roosevelt, *This Is My Story* (New York: Harper and Brothers, 1937), p. 17.

5. Ibid., pp. 17–18.

6. Paul F. Boller, Jr., *Presidential Wives: An Ancedotal History* (New York: Oxford University, 1988), p. 287.

7. Lash, p. 28.

8. Gurewitsch, p. 11.

9. Ibid.

Chapter 2

1. Joseph P. Lash, *"Life Was Meant to Be Lived,"*: *A Centenary Portrait of Eleanor Roosevelt* (New York: W.W. Norton and Co., 1984), p. 5.

2. Eleanor Roosevelt, *This Is My Story* (New York: Harper and Brothers, 1937), p. 6.

3. Ibid., p. 5.

4. Ibid., p. 1.

5. Ibid., p. 11.

6. Ibid., p. 18.

7. Blanche Weisen Cook, *Eleanor Roosevelt, Volume One: 1884–1933* (New York: Viking Press, 1992), p. 48.

8. Michael Teague, *Mrs. L.: Conversations with Alice Roosevelt Longworth* (New York: Doubleday and Company, 1981), p. 154.

9. Ibid.

10. Roosevelt, p. 19.

11. David McCullough, *Mornings on Horseback* (New York: Simon and Schuster, 1981), pp. 368–369.

12. Roosevelt, p. 34.

Chapter 3

1. Eleanor Roosevelt, *This Is My Story* (New York: Harper and Brothers, 1937), p. 51.

2. Blanche Weisen Cook, *Eleanor Roosevelt, Volume One: 1884–1933* (New York: Viking Press, 1992), p. 107.

3. Joseph P. Lash, *"Life Was Meant to Be Lived,": A Centenary Portrait of Eleanor Roosevelt* (New York: W.W. Norton and Co., 1984), p. 9.

4. Cook, p. 114.

5. Roosevelt, p. 84.

6. Cook, p. 115.

7. Roosevelt, p. 89.

8. Cook, pp. 131, 134–135.

9. Ibid., p. 135.

10. Ibid., p. 150.

11. Roosevelt, p. 126.

Chapter 4

1. Joseph P. Lash, *"Life Was Meant to Be Lived,": A Centenary Portrait of Eleanor Roosevelt* (New York: W.W. Norton and Co., 1984), p. 15.

2. Eleanor Roosevelt, *This Is My Story* (New York: Harper and Brothers, 1937), p. 145.

3. Ibid., p. 162.

4. Ibid., p. 173.

5. Joseph P. Lash, *Eleanor and Franklin* (New York: W.W. Norton and Co., 1971), p. 166.

6. Ibid.

7. Blanche Weisen Cook, *Eleanor Roosevelt, Volume One: 1884–1933* (New York: Viking Press, 1992), pp. 211–212.

8. Lash, *Eleanor and Franklin*, p. 195.

9. Ibid.

10. Ibid., p. 196.

11. Cook, p. 278.

12. Ibid.

13. Michael Teague, *Mrs. L.: Conversations with Alice Roosevelt Longworth* (New York: Doubleday and Company, 1981), p. 157.

14. Roosevelt, p. 320.

15. Lash, *Eleanor and Franklin*, pp. 220, 226.

16. Ibid., p. 226.

17. Roosevelt Campobello International Park brochure, p. 4.

Chapter 5

1. Eleanor Roosevelt, *This I Remember* (New York: Harper and Brothers, 1949), p. 25.

2. Paul F. Boller, Jr., *Presidential Wives: An Ancedotal History* (New York: Oxford University, 1988), p. 290.

3. Ibid.

4. Eleanor Roosevelt, *This Is My Story* (New York: Harper and Brothers, 1937), p. 352.

5. Blanche Weisen Cook, *Eleanor Roosevelt, Volume One: 1884–1933* (New York: Viking Press, 1992), p. 344.

6. Ibid., p. 348.

7. Roosevelt, *This Is My Story,* p. 354.

8. Cook, p. 399.

9. Joseph P. Lash, *"Life Was Meant to Be Lived,": A Centenary Portrait of Eleanor Roosevelt* (New York: W.W. Norton and Co., 1984), p. 47.

10. Roosevelt, *This I Remember,* p. 56.

Chapter 6

1. Allan Nevins and Henry Steele Commager, *A Pocket History of the United States* (New York: Pocket Books, 1981), p. 416.

2. Joseph P. Lash, *"Life Was Meant to Be Lived,": A Centenary Portrait of Eleanor Roosevelt* (New York: W.W. Norton and Co., 1984), p. 57.

3. Ibid., pp. 59–61.

4. Paul F. Boller, Jr., *Presidential Wives: An Ancedotal History* (New York: Oxford University, 1988), p. 293.

5. Eleanor Roosevelt, *This I Remember* (New York: Harper and Brothers, 1949), p. 131.

6. Ibid., p. 141.

7. Lash, p. 77.

8. Boller, p. 295.

9. Lash, p. 90.

10. Eleanor Roosevelt, *My Day, Volume I* (New York: Pharos Books, 1989), p. 113.

11. Roosevelt, *This I Remember,* pp. 219–220.

12. Roosevelt, *My Day, Volume I,* p. 224.

13. James L. Whitehead, *The Museum of the Franklin D. Roosevelt Library,* booklet, p. 12.

14. Lash, p. 114.

15. Boller, p. 299.

16. Bernard Asbell, *Mother and Daughter: The Letters of Eleanor and Anna Roosevelt* (New York: Fromm International Publishing, 1982), p. 185.

17. Boller, p. 300.

18. Asbell, pp. 189–190.

Chapter 7

1. Joseph P. Lash, *Eleanor: The Years Alone* (New York: W.W. Norton and Company, 1972), p. 15.

2. Eleanor Roosevelt, *My Day,, Volume II* (New York: Pharos Books, 1989), p. 45.

3. Eleanor Roosevelt, *On My Own: The Years Since the White House* (New York: Harper and Brothers, 1958), p. 40.

4. Ibid., pp. 40–41.

5. Ibid., p. 51.

6. Ibid.

7. Ibid., p. 52.

8. Ibid., p. 53.

9. Joseph P. Lash, *"Life Was Meant to Be Lived,"*: *A Centenary Portrait of Eleanor Roosevelt* (New York: W.W. Norton and Co., 1984), p. 134.

10. Lash, *The Years Alone*, p. 59.

11. Lash, *"Life Was Meant to Be Lived,"* p. 154.

12. Ibid., p. 157.

Chapter 8

1. Eleanor Roosevelt, *On My Own: The Years Since the White House* (New York: Harper and Brothers, 1958), p. 95.

2. Joseph P. Lash, *"Life Was Meant to Be Lived,"*: *A Centenary Portrait of Eleanor Roosevelt* (New York: W.W. Norton and Co., 1984), p. 168.

3. Joseph P. Lash, *Eleanor: The Years Alone* (New York: W.W. Norton and Company, 1972), p. 212.

4. Ibid., p. 234.

5. Ibid., p. 235.

6. Eleanor Roosevelt, *My Day, Volume II* (New York: Pharos Books, 1989), p. 226.

7. Lash, *The Years Alone*, p. 158.

8. Ibid., p. 159.

9. "Her Glow Warmed the World," *Newsweek*, November 19, 1962, p. 50.

10. Lash, *"Life Was Meant to Be Lived,"* p. 165.

11. Roosevelt, *My Day, Volume I*, p. vii.

12. Franklin D. Roosevelt Library transcript of interview with Nina Roosevelt Gibson, August 14, 1979, pp. 61–62.

13. Ibid., pp. 70–71.

14. Franklin D. Roosevelt Library transcript of interview with John R. Boettiger, August 1, 1979, pp. 10–11.

15. Ibid., p. 45.

16. Ibid.

17. Roosevelt, *On My Own*, p. 159.

18. Lash, *The Years Alone*, p. 256.

19. Roosevelt, *On My Own*, p. 175.

20. Lash, *The Years Alone*, p. 303.

21. "World Leaders Send Messages," *The New York Times*, November 9, 1962, p. 25.

22. Ibid.

23. Ibid.

24. Michael Teague, *Mrs. L.: Conversations with Alice Roosevelt Longworth* (New York: Doubleday and Company, 1981), p. 161.

25. Ibid., p. 160.

26. Carol Felsenthal, *Alice Roosevelt Longworth* (New York: G.P. Putnam's Sons, 1988), p. 219.

27. Lash, *"Life Was Meant to Be Lived,"* jacket copy.

Further Reading

Hickok, Lorena. *The Story of Eleanor Roosevelt.* Grosset & Dunlap, 1959.

Jacobs, William J. *Eleanor Roosevelt: A Life of Happiness and Tears.* New York: Marshall Cavendish, 1991.

McClure, Ruth. *Eleanor Roosevelt: An Eager Spirit.* Norton, 1984.

Roosevelt, Eleanor. *On My Own: The Years Since the White House.* New York: Harper & Brothers, 1958.

Roosevelt, Eleanor. *This I Remember.* New York: Harper and Brothers, 1949.

Roosevelt, Eleanor. *This Is My Story.* New York: Harper and Brothers, 1937.

Roosevelt, Eleanor. *The United Nations and Youth.* Doubleday & Co., 1950.

Roosevelt, Eleanor. *You Learn by Living.* Spring Arbor, 1960.

Toor, Rachel. *Eleanor Roosevelt.* New York: Chelsea House, 1989.

Will, Ann. *Eleanor Roosevelt: Courageous Girl.* Bobbs-Merrill, 1965.

Index